From
LEARNING
to
EARNING

YAHOO! hotjobs®

From
LEARNING
to
EARNING

SUCCESS STRATEGIES FOR
NEW GRADS

DAN FINNIGAN AND MARC KARASU

STERLING PUBLISHING
New York

Published by Sterling Publishing Co., Inc.
387 Park Avenue South, New York, NY 10016

Distributed in Canada by Sterling Publishing
c/o Canadian Manda Group, 165 Dufferin Street
Toronto, Ontario M6K 3H6

Distributed in Great Britain by Chrysalis Books Group PLC
The Chrysalis Building, Bramley Road, London W10 6SP, England

Distributed in Australia by Capricorn Link (Australia) Pty. Ltd.
P.O. Box 704, Windsor, NSW 2756, Australia

Library of Congress Cataloging-in-Publication Data

Finnigan, Dan.
  From learning to earning : Yahoo! HotJobs success strategies for new grads / Dan Finnigan and Marc Karasu.
      p. cm.
  ISBN 1-4027-2825-5
  1. College graduates--Employment. 2. Job hunting. 3. Success. I. Karasu, Marc.
II. Title.

HD6277.F56 2006
650.14--dc22   2005027115

Printed in the United States of America

10 9 8 7 6 5 4 3 2 1

For information about custom editions, special sales, premium and corporate purchases, please contact the Sterling Special Sales Department at 800-805-5489 or specialsales@sterlingpub.com

Cover Design: Amy King
Interior Design: Stacey May

We dedicate this book to our families
and friends for their support
and inspiration.

CONTENTS

Acknowledgments

Producing a book means relying on one of the rules we've discussed in these pages: Build and maintain your network! With that, we'd like to thank Laura Boswell, without whose dedication and expertise this book would not have been possible. We're eternally grateful for the hard work and wisdom of Project Manager Amy Werner, as well as that of our colleagues at Yahoo! HotJobs, including Douglas Lee, Sean Bosker, Lauren Meller, Yahoo! Legal, Libby Sartain, the Yahoo! Talent Acquisition Team, and our former colleagues Erin Hovanec and Christopher Jones.

We'd also like to thank the staff of Barnes & Noble Publishing, including: our editor, Meredith Peters Hale; our publisher, Michael Fragnito; Production Manager Paulette Hodge; Creative Director Jeffrey Batzli; Designer Wendy Ralphs; Managing Editor Maria Spano; Pamela Wong; and the agent for this series, John C. Leonhardt.

Many thanks to the following for their input: Susan Bixler, Laura Donovan, Lisa Gravelle, Pat Katepoo, Kate Moody, John Rogers, Mary-Frances Wain, Peter Weddle, Lou Adler, Cheryl Ferguson, and all the other executives who contributed pieces to this book. Finally, we'd like to acknowledge Stacey May and Amy King for the book's elegant and efficient design.

Introduction: Now Is the Time to Find the Right One

Are you a recent college graduate worried about entering the job market? Or perhaps you're still a student, concerned about your prospects and hoping to get a jump start on a job? Perhaps the worries of life in the "real world" have you and your classmates clinging to those simpler days of college midterms and meal plans.

Who could blame you? The headlines and unemployment reports can make the job market seem like a dark, tangled jungle in which you're a fresh piece of meat just hoping for a job that doesn't require a hairnet. It's enough to make anyone want to hole up in a dorm room for another four years.

However, there has never been a better time to be a new job seeker! Why?

YOUR PAL, THE INTERNET

You're almost certainly acquainted with the Internet—now you and this top technology tool are going to be partners in your next big endeavor, your job search. So make some coffee and find a comfortable chair—you and the Net are going to be spending a lot of time together.

You'll probably start your job search by visiting online job boards—as you should. These provide the fastest access to thousands of available jobs every day; yet their interfaces allow you to search, with near-pinpoint accuracy, for the exact type of job you want. Beefy job descriptions give you important details about each position that you can use to create highly targeted resumes and cover letters. You can then store those documents online and also network with other job seekers on message boards, sign up for free e-mail alerts that bring new jobs right to your e-mail inbox, receive free newsletters, and more.

Meanwhile, company job boards also offer job postings as well as executive biographies and insight into the company culture. You can learn before you even walk in the door whether or not you want to work there, just by a few clicks of the mouse from the comfort of your home.

Finally, Internet research sites like Yahoo! Finance (http://finance.yahoo.com/) can give you important information about a company, including stock reports, employment figures, and the latest news stories.

JOBS ARE BOOMING

Were you aware that soon there might actually be more jobs than workers to fill them? Now you can thank Mom and Dad not only for all that food, shelter, and tuition stuff—but also maybe even for your job, too!

Members of the "baby boom" generation (your parents and others born between 1946 and 1964) are already beginning to retire, and the numbers will increase dramatically as we approach 2011, when the first boomers turn sixty-five (the current retirement age).

Hey—did you just hear that *whooshing* sound? That, dear graduates, is the sound of millions of *jobs* suddenly becoming vacant! And, as you learned in Physics 101, nature abhors a vacuum. Someone will have to fill those shoes. That means you, the job seeker, will have the advantage as companies compete to woo you.

Meanwhile, forget your dad's warning about impending financial doom, the supposed college graduate career crises, and all the naysayers—there are *always* new jobs opening up, regardless of the economic situation. The most recent Bureau of Labor Statistics (BLS) ten-year outlook study for years 2002–2012 projects that U.S. jobs will grow from 144 million to 165 million. And many people are not aware of the numerous job openings that become available *each month*, even during what is perceived as a slumping job market. There is still a lot of hiring going on even when the media focuses on the latest spate of layoffs. Remember that when you feel as if no recruiter is going to call you back!

SCHOOL IS COOL

Believe it or not, simply being a college graduate offers you resources, skills, and opportunities that others don't have: internships, free career counseling, on-campus and alumni networking opportunities, the collective pity of employers who were once new grads seeking their first jobs too. . .

And education pays. That diploma you're holding may have cost a pretty penny, but it can help you make one too! Higher levels of education are generally associated with higher earnings and lower incidences of unemployment. According to the BLS, in 2003 alone, the unemployment rate for those twenty-five and under with a bachelor's degree was only 3.3 percent, and they earned a median income of $900 per week! By comparison, high school graduates with no college degree had a 5.5 percent unemployment rate and averaged just $554 per week.

In addition, college graduates who become unemployed are generally unemployed for shorter periods. College graduates are also more likely to receive employer-sponsored training than workers with less education—a major asset in an economy in which the skills in demand are constantly evolving.

So be proud of that degree—and always look for new ways to build on it!

FIND THE RIGHT ONE

Yes, a job search can seem daunting. Will you find your dream job, or will you be flipping burgers at a restaurant that makes you wear suspenders with "flair"? How long will it take to get an offer? Will it be the "right offer"?

But you should be *excited*, not afraid! A wonderful world of opportunities awaits you—even if it takes you a while to find them. Be patient and realistic—and don't be afraid to explore different opportunities and industries.

This book aims to help you in your search. We cover everything from assessing which job is right for you, to creating an attention-grabbing resume, to evaluating a company's offer. For additional resources, at the end of each chapter you'll find recommended Web sites from the experts at Yahoo! HotJobs and suggested reading from the editors at Barnes & Noble.

Jobs are developing, even increasing over the next decade—and college graduates will reap those benefits. Also, you have enthusiasm, a fresh outlook, and a willingness to learn that employers seek and companies need to thrive and remain competitive in a global economy.

So think of being a new job seeker as a help, not a hindrance. Now is *your* time to *find the right one*!

CHAPTER 1

Assess Yourself: Discover Your Skills and Career Goals

B. Smaller

"Actually, I'm hoping what I'm going to be when I grow up hasn't been invented yet."

Imagine you're in fifth-century Athens. The great philosopher Socrates stands in the middle of a circle of eager students, each shouting over the next to be heard. The voices suddenly quiet down when one student raises his hand and asks the question that has plagued human beings since the dawn of time: "How do I find a job with no experience?"

It's quite possible that Socrates paused, stroked his beard, and then stated his now-famous quote—"Know thyself"—as the answer. He understood that knowing yourself is one of the most important keys to a happy life—much of which comes from finding a fulfilling career.

Chances are you're asking the same question. But you have more experience than you think! Life is work—after all, you've been employed at it for a lifetime, so you must be doing something right. Of course, work experience is important, but there is much more that counts in the workplace. By "knowing yourself," you stand a much better chance of finding a career that you love, and more quickly, too.

When you understand your own passions, preferences, gripes, fears, and influences, your path through life will be much smoother. Knowing yourself tells you what situations to avoid, what goals to pursue, what traits you need to downplay or amplify, which people make you happy, or miserable, and, hopefully, what work you find enjoyable and fulfilling.

LIST YOUR SKILLS

Skills and traits fall into numerous categories, but to keep things simple we'll put them into two groups: **hard** and **soft** skills.

Hard Skills

You only need to read any job ad to get an idea of what hard skills are. These are the measurable talents and/or certifications you have built either by hands-on practice or training: Excel, Web development, public speaking, Spanish, computer programming, and so on.

If you're currently in or have completed college, you already have a number of hard skills you can list on your resume; in addition to the above, these may include researching, budgeting, and familiarity with Mac and/or Microsoft, just to name a few. You've learned these skills in your classes and computer labs, clubs, sports, sororities and fraternities, volunteer experiences, summer jobs, and internships.

▶**Action Items:** Write down five of your hard skills. Think about the jobs for which these skills might qualify you.

1. _____

2. _____

3. _____

4. _____

5. _____

Now that you've identified some of your hard skills, there are a few things to remember. First, just because you are good at something doesn't mean that's what you will enjoy or are destined to do the rest of your life. You might be very good at math, but that doesn't mean you'd be happy as an accountant. You might have aced every chemistry test you ever took, but you might not enjoy a life spent in the lab.

Second, hard skills tend to be skills that most people, if they apply themselves, can learn. That's the good news about hard skills—even if you don't have the ones you need now, you can generally acquire them if you have the time and patience.

The bad news is that hard skills alone don't distinguish you from others. Many people can run a server, speak French, or work with spreadsheets. How do you set yourself apart? That's where soft skills come in.

Soft Skills

The beginning of this job ad sounds like a cliché:

> *"Seeking hard-working, self-starter with leadership skills and discipline for entry-level sales job..."*

This description doesn't say much about the job itself, but it does tell you that certain intangible qualities—soft skills—are important to this employer.

While soft skills can be learned, more often than not they are something you were born with a knack for: attention to detail, strong communication skills, team building, and so on.

Soft skills are the secret to finding a job without prior work experience. You may not have many hard skills, but you can make up for that with good communication skills, the ability to meet deadlines, or creative problem solving.

In his popular books, *Emotional Intelligence: Why It Can Matter More Than IQ* and *Working With Emotional Intelligence,* psychologist and former *New York Times* reporter Daniel Goleman argues that it's not your intellect, experience, or tangible skills that make you successful, but rather your emotional intelligence, or how well you can "read" other people and relate to them. Goleman even argues that "EI" matters twice as much as IQ or technical skills in job success!

▶**Action Items:** Write down five soft skills you have acquired from past work, school, or life experience:

1. _____

2. _____

3. _____

4. _____

5. _____

⋯·T̠H̠I̠N̠K̠ Outside the Box 💡

Soft Skills for the Rest of Us

If you're entering the working world for the first time later in life or after an extended absence, you're probably full of soft skills. You just have to figure out what they are and learn how to present them.

Maybe you showed leadership in starting a neighborhood watch program. Perhaps you demonstrated negotiating skills when choosing a contractor to renovate your home. Or, better yet, perhaps you took initiative and did the renovation yourself.

Think about your life experience and the obstacles you've faced—how did you get around them? What skills did you use?

CAREER ASSESSMENT

Now that you've listed some hard and soft skills, you have a good baseline from which to begin your job search.

First you need to begin narrowing down the possibilities. The key? "Know thyself."

Consider the things that make a position or field right for you. For this you'll need to examine various factors such as **personality, interests, "work quirks,"** and **values**.

▶Action Items: Take Stock of Your Talents

Many of us lack insight about our talents. Look for these five clues:

☼ **Yearning.** What kinds of activities are you drawn to?

☼ **Rapid Learning.** What kinds of activities do you seem to pick up quickly?

☼ **Flow.** In what activities did the steps just come to you automatically, without a lot of coaching?

☼ **Glimpses of Excellence.** When have you had moments of triumph and thought, "How did I do that?"

☼ **Satisfaction.** What activities give you a kick, either when you are doing them or immediately after finishing them?

Once you focus on how your natural talents make you unique, it becomes easier to articulate these strengths to other people. Vividly and coherently describing how you have been successful in the past, what motivates you, how you get things done, how you solve problems, and how you relate to other people will allow you to stand out among job seekers. (Exercise courtesy of the Gallup Organization.)

▶Action Items: Past Personal Success, Future Career Triumph

Look to your greatest successes for clues to the right career. To help you think about your successes, ask yourself:

☼ What has been my most successful experience in an employment, service, or volunteer work setting?

☼ What has been my most successful experience in an academic, learning, or athletic setting?

☼ What has been my greatest success in an interpersonal relationship, leadership role, club, team, or organization?

Then focus on each success, one at a time. Relive the experience in your mind and ask yourself:

☼ What was it about this experience that makes it stand out as one of my greatest successes?

☼ What did I do that contributed to producing this success?

☼ What was my mental approach to this success?

☼ Which talents contributed to producing this success?

☼ What do I want to take from this success and make sure it is part of my career-planning process?

(Exercise courtesy of the Gallup Organization.)

Personality

Don't overlook your personality when beginning your job search. Your personality is the sum of the distinctive inner qualities that make up who you are as a person. It can provide a framework for helping you decide which industry or occupation is the best fit for you.

For example, if you're outgoing and a good communicator, you might be a great public relations professional or salesperson. If you're precise and enjoy getting the right result every time, you might have a knack for finance or engineering. If you're a good listener and enjoy helping people better their lives, you might consider social work.

▶**Action Items:** List five of your personality traits (think "outgoing," "energetic," "sensitive," and so forth):

1. _____

2. _____

3. _____

4. _____

5. _____

Now write down five careers where these traits might apply:

1. _____

2. _____

3. _____

4. _____

5. _____

Here are just a few examples of personality traits and careers with which they correspond:

Compassionate: nurse, doctor, veterinarian, social worker, minister
Artistic: painter, musician, producer, writer
Assertive: teacher, lawyer, politician, salesperson
Extraverted: event planner, public relations professional
Precise: scientist, researcher, engineer, architect, pilot
Articulate: writer, motivational speaker, journalist
Fearless: actor, member of the military, law enforcement officer
Patient: special education teacher, counselor

Interests

Your interests are the hobbies and skills you have developed on your own because you wanted to, and not because you were paid or forced to work on them as part of a class. Perhaps you have a natural gift for them. They might be, in fact, the very things you would want to do with your life if money were not a factor.

Your interests can give you many options for job choices: If you enjoy sewing, you might like a job in the fashion industry or running a fabrics store. If you like to cook, you could be a chef or work in restaurant management. If you like travel, you might enjoy working as a travel agent or in a PR agency that promotes cruise lines.

▶**Action Items:** To get a better idea of your interests, ask yourself these questions :

☼ What was I doing the last time I completely lost track of time?

☼ If I could do anything I wanted and be paid for it, what would it be?

☼ My ideal weekend is spent doing _____.

▶**Action Items:** List five of your interests (think "scuba diving" or "knitting"):

1. _____

2. _____

3. _____

4. _____

5. _____

Now write down five careers that would let you pursue these interests.

1. _____

2. _____

3. _____

4. _____

5. _____

"Work Quirks"

"Work quirks" are those little things you need from a job's culture and environment to do your best work. Even if you like a particular group of people, college class, or job, the "little things" (your coworker's bad breath, a friend who interrupts, a professor who is readily available for help) are ultimately what make you love them or leave them.

When you picture yourself in your new job, what do you see? Do you like a work environment that is bustling and chaotic or quiet, with people keeping mostly to themselves? Do you want to be able to dress casually for work or do you prefer a more professional environment? Do you like your supervisors to "keep an eye" on your projects, or do you work better without supervision?

Certain industries are known for their own quirks. Investment banking often draws those who like a fast-paced, high-pressure, and conservative environment. Publishing, however, is usually more creative, flexible, and relaxed. And sales attracts those who thrive in a competitive, energetic, and gregarious environment.

Every company is different—and so is every job. As a relatively new job seeker, you may have to be more flexible about your work quirks in order to find a first job. But you do want to try to find a workplace in which you are comfortable and productive. Knowing your work quirks can make your job more fulfilling— especially if the work itself is not quite what you want to be doing.

▶**Action Items:** Write five of your "work quirks," and consider which career fields/ jobs might or might not have them.

Work Quirks

1. _____

2. _____

3. _____

4. _____

5. _____

Applicable Fields/Jobs

1. _____

2. _____

3. _____

4. _____

5. _____

Values

Values consist of what you believe regarding work, religion, politics, social consciousness, family priorities, and the like. They are the things that "little voice" inside your head nags you about (and usually for good reason!).

Consider your values and how far you are willing to bend, if at all, to find a job. Once you start down a career path ignoring your values—say, taking a job for money alone, or selling a product you know to be faulty—it can be very hard to get back on course down the road. For example, Meredith, a college senior, interviewed with a law firm in Washington, DC, and loved everything about it— except the firm's reputation for representing tobacco companies. Given her strong opinions about the health risks associated with smoking, she would not have felt right working on such cases—and she explained this to her interviewer. Meredith didn't get the job, but she didn't regret sticking to her principles. As she summed it up: "Ultimately, I never would have been happy there, and it would have shown in my work."

▶**Action Items:** List your five most strongly held values (qualities such as "honesty," "giving back to the community," or "protecting the environment"):

1. _____

2. _____

3. _____

4. _____

5. _____

Now list five things you absolutely won't tolerate in a job (a dishonest service, a poor environmental record, a dangerous product, prejudice):

1. _____

2. _____

3. _____

4. _____

5. _____

Company Values

You're likely to be more satisfied and rewarded by work at a company that you respect. Company values took center stage in the early twenty-first century after a number of high-profile scandals left thousands of workers stranded with no jobs and no retirement income.

What their leaders do, how they make their products, how public companies invest their earnings—all are indicative of a company's values.

Fortunately there is much information about companies online. To locate a company's Web site, just type the name of the company into Yahoo! (www.yahoo.com). Once you find the home page, look for a link that says "About Us" or "Company Info" and read all the information you can find. Browse through the rest of the site, including pages such as "Mission," "Management," "Press Releases," and "Contact Us."

You can conduct in-depth research on sites such as Yahoo! Finance (http://finance.yahoo.com) and Hoover's (www.hoovers.com). PR Newswire (www.prnewswire.com) and Business Wire (www.businesswire.com) are good sources for recent and objective company news.

Last, you can look in magazines, newspapers (either in print or online) and blogs for information that can help you understand a company's values and whether they are a good fit for you.

ASSESSMENT TESTS

MBTI…ENFP—they sound like they could be television networks, but they actually have to do with assessing your personality, interests, values, soft skills, and work quirks. These tests can help pinpoint career fields that are right for you.

From the Desk of

Andrew C. Taylor
Chairman and Chief Executive Officer, Enterprise Rent-A-Car

At sixteen years old, I started out in the family business by spending my summer and holiday vacations washing cars, answering the phone, and helping customers at the company that was then known as Executive Leasing. Today, Enterprise Rent-A-Car has grown to become North America's largest rental car company.

In the more than thirty years I've worked for the company, I've never forgotten the lesson I learned back at the beginning: Success lies in a willingness to pitch in and do whatever needs to be done, combined with a commitment to getting the little things right. No task is insignificant if it contributes to a satisfied customer who comes back again and again.

For those taking their first steps into the workplace, my advice would be to find opportunities to learn your chosen field from the ground up—to embrace and understand all those little things that add up to success, for you and for the organization. At Enterprise, we believe this so strongly, that virtually every member of our senior management team started out as I did, serving customers at the counter and learning the frontline nuts and bolts of our business. In fact, to this day, the thousands of management trainees who join our team each year—all of them college-educated—begin their Enterprise careers the same way.

So, as you make the transition from your education to your career, view your early work experiences as a chance to gain a more thorough understanding of business. And use those learning experiences as a chance to develop those qualities employers value, such as integrity, enthusiasm, dependability, leadership, and drive. In my experience, it's by bringing those qualities to your earliest duties and responsibilities that you demonstrate your potential for bigger things.

There are a variety of exercises and tests that can help you more formally understand your personality and inner qualities. You can take them through your college's career services office, employment agencies, career counseling firms, your local adult education center, or libraries.

If cost is prohibitive, there are also Web sites and books with these tests (we list a few at the end of this chapter). You won't get a professional's interpretation, but they can give you an idea of where you stand.

The following are some of the most popular tests.

Myers-Briggs Type Indicator (also known as MBTI, Myers-Briggs-Jung, or Jung-Myers-Briggs)

This test is pretty much the Homecoming Queen of all personality tests. Based on the work of pioneer psychologist Carl G. Jung and created by Isabel Myers Briggs, the MBTI is intended to measure a person's preferences using four basic scales:

- ☼ Extraversion/Introversion
- ☼ Sensing/Intuitive
- ☼ Thinking/Feeling
- ☼ Judging/Perceiving

The various combinations of these preferences result in sixteen personality types, typically denoted by four letters—for example, ENFP (Extraversion, Intuitive, Feeling, and Perceiving)—to represent a person's tendencies on the four scales.

The ENFP, for example, often possesses the following qualities:

- ☼ Warm and bright
- ☼ Great at starting projects, but sometimes lacks follow-through
- ☼ Unusually broad range of interests and talents
- ☼ Gets bored easily
- ☼ Wants to please people
- ☼ Enjoys being the center of attention

Therefore, ENFPs are said to be best fit for careers like journalism, acting, human resources, and marketing.

From the Desk of

Donald J. Trump
Star of *The Apprentice*

The best piece of career advice I ever received came from my father, Fred Trump. He told me: "Know everything you can about what you're doing." I would say the same thing to every person embarking on a career or a job search. You must know what you're doing and what you're going after. This may involve a lot of research and painstaking work on your part, but it is absolutely necessary and will save you, and others, a lot of time in the long run.

One of the most off-putting scenarios for me as an executive is when someone comes in with a vague idea of what he's doing or what he'd like to be doing. I want people who know what they're doing and why they're doing it. Otherwise, they are wasting my time as well as their own. Focus yourself before going out on interviews, and don't expect others to focus for you. You will not only fail to impress them, you might also wind up irritating them. How many of you would hire some-one who has already managed to irritate you during the interview?

I like to know why someone thinks he or she is the best person for the job. Could you tell me succinctly why you are the best person for me to hire? Could you convince me of this in less than thirty seconds? Would you be able to defend yourself against any questions of your merit that I might have? Can you promote yourself in a way that is not egotistical but simply factual? Ask yourself these questions before going on any interview, and you will be going a long way toward preparing yourself. Good luck, work hard, and never give up.

Keirsey Temperament Sorter

The Keirsey uses the results of the Myers-Briggs to assign you to one of four different "temperaments"—predispositions toward certain attitudes and actions. The temperaments are artists, guardians, idealists, and rationals. These are then further divided into classifications that include "champion," "counselor," "supervisor," and "performer." The test is intended to increase self-awareness, improve decision-making skills, enhance business and personal relationships, and improve communication skills.

Bar-On EQ-I
Dr. Reuven Bar-On coined the term "EQ" and developed this test to provide a measure of overall emotional intelligence. It covers fifteen different emotional skill areas found to be most important in successfully coping with life's demands. These factors are clustered into various categories such as intrapersonal, interpersonal, adaptability, stress management, and general mood.

RIASEC
Dr. John Holland's popular test is based on six types—Realistic, Investigative, Artistic, Social, Enterprising, or Conventional. This test is used to match personality types to possible careers.

These tests are merely approximate measurements of your personality, soft skills, and values—their results don't mean you are definitely one type of person or another. Regardless of what a test might tell you, don't be afraid to think big. Just because you are good at writing does not mean you can't be good at numbers, too. Use the results as a guideline, but don't take them too seriously.

▶Action Items: Kidding Around
Think back to when you were a child—many times, the things we enjoyed doing as children give insight into what we really feel fulfilled with—and therefore what jobs we'd be happy doing—before the world has a chance to steer us differently.

Write down some of your first happy memories. What were the things that interested you? Yeah, sure, you can list Barbie dolls and Tonka trucks, but think beyond that. What movies fascinated you—science fiction or musicals? Did you like to read? Did you enjoy playing with siblings or alone? What could you do for hours and be completely entertained?

Now study the list—do you spot any trends? Is there an activity you would love to start doing again? Can these discoveries be reconciled with some "real-world" jobs? Keep this list nearby to refer back to as you read this book.

▶Action Items: R.I.P. (Rest in Prosperity)
Now let's fast-forward about ninety years—and write your obituary! What would it say? Take some time to write a few paragraphs summing up your life—particularly where work is concerned. What were your accomplishments? Your interests? What

legacy did you leave behind? How do your future accomplishments relate, if at all, to your childhood interests and your current interests and studies? Consider your future as you proceed through this book—it's never too soon to set goals.

We hope this chapter has helped you discover some of your hard and soft skills—as well as your career preferences and goals—and begin to categorize them as you start you job search. In the next chapter, we will explore the basics of the hiring process. We'll also talk about what you can expect once you begin seeking a job where you can apply these hard and soft skills.

Recommended Books

Emotional Intelligence: Why It Can Matter More Than IQ by Daniel Goleman (Bantam Books, ISBN 0553375067, $17.00).

Working With Emotional Intelligence by Daniel Goleman (Bantam Doubleday Dell Publishing Group, ISBN 0553104624, $28.00).

What Should I Do with My Life? The True Story of People Who Answered the Ultimate Question by Po Bronson, (Random House, Inc., ISBN 0375758984, $14.95).

Do What You Are: Discover the Perfect Career for You through the Secrets of Personality Type by Paul D. Tieger & Barbara Barron-Tieger (Little, Brown & Company, ISBN 0316880655, $18.95).

Discover What You're Best At: A Complete Career System That Lets You Test Yourself to Discover Your Own True Career Abilities by Linda Gale (Simon & Schuster, ISBN 0684839563, $14.00).

Please Understand Me: Character and Temperament Types by David Keirsey & Marilyn Bates (Prometheus Nemesis Book Company, Inc., ISBN 0960695400, $11.95).

College Majors Handbook with Real Career Paths and Payoffs: The Actual Jobs, Earnings, and Trends for Graduates of 60 College Majors by Neeta P. Fogg, Paul E. Harrington & Thomas F. Harrington (JIST Works, Inc., ISBN 1593570740, $24.95).

Recommended Web Sites

Yahoo! HotJobs—Assessments:
http://hotjobs.yahoo.com/assessment

Assessment.com:
www.assessment.com

Find Your Spot:
www.findyourspot.com

Humanmetrics—Jung Typology Test:
www.humanmetrics.com/cgi-win/JTypes1.htm

The Temperament Sorter II (registration required):
www.advisorteam.com/temperament_sorter

Queendom—Career Tests:
www.queendom.com/tests/career

Test Café—Career Tests:
www.testcafe.com/career.html

Hoovers.com:
www.hoovers.com

PR Newswire:
www.prnewswire.com

Business Wire:
www.businesswire.com

2

The (Really) Great Divide: Understanding the Hiring Process

"We have only jobs here, Mr. Sanderson, not 'gigs.'"

When it comes to the hiring process, there is a massive disconnect between job seekers and recruiters.

A recent Yahoo! HotJobs poll asked job seekers, "Do you feel you understand how the hiring process works?" The majority, 62 percent, replied "Yes."

But when we asked recruiters a similar question—"Do you feel that job seekers understand the hiring process?"—a whopping 75 percent responded "No."

That's just the tip of the iceberg. At Yahoo! HotJobs, we get thousands of e-mails from job seekers who feel lost in the hiring process:

- ☼ "I have a viable network, I have applied with several search firms, I hit the Internet and newspaper daily, and still no luck. I have been searching for the right fit for seven months now. Before my MBA I lacked current skills, now with my MBA I am overqualified . . . sheesh."

- ☼ "I am a recent graphic design graduate with a bachelor's degree. I am creative, educated, and I have good ideas. I am willing to start from the bottom and work my way up in a company . . . and I have no job. What am I doing wrong?"

- ☼ "After replying to a job ad in the paper or on the Net by faxing or emailing my resume (as instructed by the ad), is it customary to follow up with a phone call? I don't want to sound too pushy on the phone, but I would like to know where I stand."

The confusion is understandable. The hiring process is more convoluted than it appears, especially to a newbie. It's much more than going on an interview and waiting for a phone call. There are other factors you need to understand if doors are going to open for you.

So in this chapter, let's take a look at how the hiring process works, who are the people involved—and how you can use what you know about their roles to get your name to the top of their list!

BEHIND THE HIRING PROCESS "CURTAIN"

We all know the endearing scene from *The Wizard of Oz* when the "wizard" is discovered to be merely a frightened little man trying desperately to convince people he is important and all-powerful.

That's how you might view a future employer: as some kind of evil giant, determined to make you feel insignificant and small, and with a hiring process designed to hurt you, not hire you.

From the Desk of

Robert J. Stevens
President and CEO, Lockheed Martin Corporation

Now that you've finally got that diploma in hand, you're probably wondering: Where do I go from here? If you're a little intimidated right now—with the array of options and the level of competition you see—don't worry. We've all been where you are today. Over time, things sort themselves out. You'll find your place. You'll make your contribution. You'll find happiness and success. That's not me speculating—that is, in fact, what surveys of American workers consistently say.

So, relax. Take a deep breath. And spend a few minutes thinking about how your interests and competencies line up with the needs of the American (and even the world's) economy.

I've had a number of jobs in my career—starting on the factory floor and working my way up to a level of responsibility I never could have imagined in my youth. I have learned much in my journey, but the most helpful advice I can offer is fairly simple: When an opportunity presented itself, I thought beyond "What can this job do for me?" to "What can I do in the job to make this enterprise more successful?"

In hiring, one of the key characteristics I look for is a commitment to teamwork. Thousands of very talented people have to do their jobs perfectly in order for a satellite to be launched into proper orbit, or for an aircraft to safely complete its mission, or for a complex IT system to operate with extraordinary efficiency, accuracy, and reliability.

Ours is a business where lives are literally on the line and where mistakes can cost billions of dollars. We look for people who embrace challenges and have a passion for invention. We look for people from diverse backgrounds who share the common values of ethics and integrity. In the end, either we all succeed together—or we all fall short.

So when that first promising opportunity presents itself, ask yourself: Do my skills and interests line up with the needs of the organization? Do I believe in the mission of the enterprise? And will I be able to work with others so that "our success" becomes more important than "my success"? If you can answer "yes" to all those questions, jump on it—and begin your journey toward achieving the American Dream.

take a memo

Hiring Manager Myths

Myth	Reality
Loves to make me wait.	Juggling a busy schedule.
Can't keep job seekers straight.	Trying to find the "right one."
Impersonal or rude.	Hiring isn't his usual job.
Would never hire little ol' me.	He wouldn't have contacted me if I had no chance.
She's watching everything I do.	She's probably thinking about lunch.

In reality, employers are human beings; like the wizard, they are seemingly giant and fearsome, but they are actually just hoping to find some good help.

There is much at stake for the employer in the hiring process, and the responsibilities of recruiters and hiring managers go much further than just writing good job postings (and even that can be a difficult task!). Hiring ain't cheap—the Society for Human Resources Management (SHRM) estimates that the departure of a good employee costs the company around one and a half times that employee's annual salary. (We bet you had no idea you were so valuable!) Worse, a bad hire can cost even more—financially, as well as legally.

So remember as you begin the job search process that the company has a lot to consider as it views candidates. Believe it or not, they want to impress you—yes, *you*, the great, skilled, personable, qualified candidate—because a great, skilled, personable, qualified candidate can go a long way toward improving a company and its bottom line.

THE DATING, ER, HIRING GAME

As you enter the hiring process, think of it less as an audition and more like a first date with a company to see if both of you are a good fit.

First let's meet the people involved and discuss their various roles in the hiring process.

The Matchmaker (The Recruiter)

The recruiter is a hiring specialist who works with a hiring manager to bring two people, you and the hiring manager, together to work happily ever after. (Or at least for a year or two.) Her duties are many: gathering the requested skills, creating the job posting, screening resumes, scheduling interviews, helping the candidate navigate the hiring process, and making the offer. In smaller companies she may wear even more hats.

That Special Someone (The Hiring Manager)

The hiring manager is that person on whom you hope to make a great impression so he'll want to keep you around. Actually, *hiring manager* is not an official job title. Rather, it's a role supervisors perform when a position opens up in their

take a memo

Avoid Q&A Faux Pas at the Job Interview

Job candidates who confuse the roles of recruiter and hiring manager often ask the wrong question of the wrong person and wind up ruining otherwise great interviews. We'll discuss interviewing in detail in chapter 9, but here are some guidelines:

The **recruiter** is your general resource for company information. Ask him or her about employee benefits, including health insurance and 401(k) plans. Don't ask about vacation this early in the search—it can leave a bad impression.

Since the recruiter oversees the administrative duties associated with filling open positions, you might want to ask her about the next steps in the process. The recruiter will also be able to tell you who your primary contact will be. Make sure you get this person's name, title, phone number, and e-mail address.

The **hiring manager** is the ideal person to answer any questions you have about the specifics of the position, including the day-to-day responsibilities. You should also ask intelligent questions that demonstrate that you have researched the company and, if possible, the group the hiring manager oversees. Be prepared to show an understanding of what the company does—if the company has a Web site, spend some time there reading bios of senior management and recent press releases. Avoid asking questions about benefits—these should be reserved for the recruiter.

department. While filling the job, they still maintain their regular jobs in the company. Therefore, hiring managers have a limited amount of time to spend on *hiring*. And because they aren't trained human resources professionals, much like a nervous first date, they might not be at their best when you meet them—so cut 'em a little slack, okay?

Meet the Parent (The Boss' Boss)

The boss' boss wants to make sure her pride and joy, the hiring manager, is associating with qualified candidates. You may meet her at some point during the hiring process. (Just be sure to be polite and have your hiring manager home by twelve—he has work to do.)

The Friends (Coworkers)

Just as a date might solicit input about you from his buddies after you've met them, a hiring manager might have you speak with some of your potential coworkers. They may not have good interviewing skills, but their opinions of your personality and enthusiasm will count, so put your best foot forward.

FOR LOVE AND MONEY

Comparing the hiring process to dating might sound worrisome: No one likes having to impress people, wondering when or whether to call, or agonizing

take a memo

Initial Screening Questions

The following are some questions you might encounter in an initial screening phone call or application/questionnaire:

Why are you applying for a job with our company?

What are your salary requirements?

What is your greatest strength?

What is your greatest weakness?

Describe a difficult situation you encountered and how you handled it.

How did you hear about this position?

What interests you about this position?

about wearing the right clothes or the many other small, but crucial, details that can lead to a significant other—or to another Saturday night alone. If it's any consolation, the recruiter and the hiring manager have quite a bit to worry about, too!

The hiring process actually begins even before you enter the picture. First, the hiring manager lets the recruiter know she needs to fill a position. They work together to come up with the proper skills, level, title, and possibly salary/benefits to list in the job posting. The recruiter will then post the job online and/or in a newspaper.

Next, you spot the listing and submit your resume and cover letter for the job. The first person to receive that information is the recruiter. She will screen all the incoming resumes (sometimes hundreds, depending on the job and the size of the company) for the ones that best fit the desired skills and experience—as well as those with the best organization and grammar.

If you make the cut, you'll receive a call from the recruiter. If she does a phone screen, she'll ask you basic questions about your skills and interest in the position. If there is a potential match, she will arrange an in-person interview for you with the hiring manager. Or, she may just skip the phone screen and set up an interview right away.

GOIN' TO THE CHAPEL

When you interview, the recruiter will again be your first contact, your guide through the hiring process. After an initial meeting, she will take you to meet the hiring manager—your potential new boss. After a few minutes of chitchat (which is still important time—relax and be personable, but remain professional!), the hiring manager will likely ask you deeper questions about what you can do for the department and the company, and what your long-term goals are.

From there you might be finished, or you might meet the hiring manager's boss and other coworkers. If these interviews go well, there might be a second or third interview, if necessary.

Over the next few days or weeks, the recruiter will be checking your references—calling the list of professors and former supervisors you have provided to confirm that you would be a worthy employee. If those go well, further checks might be performed, such as a credit check, a background check, and even a drug test. The recruiter will also meet with the hiring manager for his thoughts and selections for the position.

Assuming you meet all of these requirements, you have proven your worth as a "suitor" at last. The recruiter will contact you and present you with an offer likely consisting of a compensation/benefits package and a formal offer letter. You then negotiate, if necessary, and/or accept the offer, both verbally and in writing (or reject the offer by phone—see more on this in chapter 11).

THE WAITING GAME

We've all been there in the dating world... We meet someone, go out, have a great time, and then...nothing. It's even worse when your next month's rent depends on hearing from the recruiter that you've been hired. You gave a great interview, your resume was impeccable...what gives?

Well, don't panic yet. The average job search can take four to six months (according to various sources such as Bankrate.com and a 2004 study conducted by outplacement company Challenger, Gray & Christmas). Granted, you're not the average candidate. But recruiters and hiring managers get detained with other duties. Much like that great date you had last Saturday, if he promised to call "in a couple of days," that doesn't necessarily mean two days.

While waiting to hear back from the recruiter, keep searching. Too often, job seekers hang their hopes on one potential job, for which they believe the interview process has gone flawlessly. Then, they wait for that position while letting other opportunities slip away—and ultimately they don't get the job after all.

Also, any number of other things could have happened. The hiring manager probably has other people to interview. Or he could have hired someone else, or decided to hire internally. This is a common practice: A job is posted publicly (by law at some organizations, such as government agencies, it must be), but a candidate within the company is promoted to the position.

Fair? Not always. But that's just one of many mysterious bumps you might encounter on the road to your first job.

Perhaps due to budget cutbacks or other scheduling changes, new hires are pushed back to the next quarter. Maybe the company is undergoing a reorganization. Maybe the hiring manager himself was laid off.

Unfortunately, you won't know this unless a company representative contacts you—or you contact one of them.

Is It OK to Call?

Yes. But, just as in dating, *within reason*. The day after you interview? No. But after a week? Certainly, especially if the hiring manager was to give you a decision by that time.

Also keep in mind when or if he said he would contact you. It's fine to (briefly) call to see where things stand. Again, these are human beings who understand that you need a livelihood—and to know whether or not it will come from their company. If the recruiter puts you off or won't give you a final answer, then the company may not have been a good fit for you in the first place.

If you are apprehensive about calling, e-mail can be a tad less intrusive. Send a brief message such as, "Hello, I am following up on my interview with John Jones on July 25. I enjoyed meeting all of you and was wondering if there was any other information I could provide you, or if you have made your decision."

The important point is, while you are waiting, keep searching! Don't stop sending out resumes, checking job postings, networking, and improving your resume and other documents in your personal portfolio. Even if you are offered the job for which you interviewed, you may not like the compensation package, or you might find something even better in the meantime. Never stop looking for the best job for you!

Recommended Books

Getting a Job (Barnes & Noble Basics Series) by Janet Garber (Silver Lining Books, ISBN 0760740240, $9.95).

201 Best Questions to Ask on Your Interview by John Kador (The McGraw-Hill Companies, ISBN 0071387730, $12.95).

How to Interview Like a Top MBA: Job Winning Strategies from Career Counselors, Recruiters, and Fortune 100 Executives by Shelly Leanne (The McGraw-Hill Companies, ISBN 007141827X, $12.95).

Road to CEO: The World's Leading Executive Recruiters Identify the Traits You Need to Make It to the Top by Sharon Voros (Adams Media Corporation, ISBN 1580623263, $20.00).

Insider's Guide to Finding a Job: Expert Advice from America's Top Employers and Recruiters by Wendy S. Enelow & Shelly Goldman (JIST Works, Inc., ISBN 1593570775, $12.95).

Recommended Web Sites

Freed Hardeman University: Questions Recruiters May Ask:
www.fhu.edu/crc/AlumniCareer_helpfulhints_EducAskYou.asp

Top Candidate Background Check:
http://hotjobs.choicetrust.com

Experían Online Credit Reports:
www.experian.com

Equifax:
www.equifax.com

CHAPTER 3

Golden Opportunities: Getting Your Foot in the Door

"Hello! What's this?"

Did you spend a bit more time in the keg line than the classroom your senior year? Due to family responsibilities, money issues, part-time jobs, or any other factors, are your final grades not quite what you had hoped?

Or perhaps you ended college months ago, and you've now returned from your backpacking trek across India, ready to settle down and find that perfect job. But as you sit in your old bedroom in your parents' house, you're starting to wish you had taken the classified ads along on your journey.

What's going to help set you apart in the job hunt, not only from experienced job seekers, but from all the other new or recent grads and entry-level job seekers like yourself?

In this chapter we'll take a look at opportunities and resources both for students who still have some time left within their institution's hallowed halls, for those who have graduated and are staring at the bedroom walls—and for every other new job seeker. We'll show why these opportunities are so important—and how to capitalize on them.

CAREER CENTERS

The importance of campus career centers really cannot be overstated for college students, recent grads, and even alumni. The very reason they exist is to help you find a career you will love. Career centers offer a wealth of valuable information, resources, and personal feedback.

The career center is your first place to begin looking for—yes!—*available jobs!* The career center is usually the first point of contact for companies with entry-level jobs or internship programs. Also, many career centers compile job opportunities in weekly e-mails to students. Make sure your name is on the career center's contact list—read applicable alerts and check the center's bulletin boards.

The career center will also have information on upcoming job fairs in fields that interest you.

Not certain what type of field is right for you? The career center will have information on assessments (personality tests, vocational aptitude tests, and so forth) to guide you. Or, perhaps you are considering graduate school instead? Again, the career center should be your first stop for information on schools, financial assistance, and the required testing (MCAT, LSAT, and the like).

Your career counseling staff can also help you develop the crucial job seeking skills that you will need as you enter the job search: resume writing, composing cover letters, interviewing. They not only will help you write the dreaded documents, but they also have books and resources to guide you. They can also give you a real live person with whom you can practice interview questions and answers.

And finally, on a deeper level, college career counselors often have degrees in (guess what) . . . *counseling*. Not only can they help you wade through the different fields you find yourself drawn to—or help if you haven't found any you like yet—but they also can give you objective help as to why you are leaning in certain directions: Do you want to be a doctor because you are great at math and science and have a compassionate personality, or only because your mom and dad are doctors, too?

hot facts

Come On: The Walk Isn't That Far!

While 41 percent of job seekers surveyed in Yahoo! HotJobs' College Community (http://community.hotjobs.com/hj-college) have visited their college career center, 43 percent haven't—but want to. So what are you waiting for?

INTERNSHIPS

Internships, which are unpaid or paid apprenticeship positions in an organization, are the Holy Grail for college students and entry-level job seekers looking for work. Internships are different from regular entry-level jobs in that the position usually emphasizes learning and "real-world" experience for the intern. Generally arranged through college career services offices (but also landed by contacting a company directly), internships are easily attainable—with a little foresight—and provide just about everything a regular job would, including:

- ☼ **Real-world work experience.** Internships give you the hands-on work experience you'll need on your resume. It doesn't matter if the "work" is faxing and filing, or helping a judge prepare her daily docket; it gives you a taste of the real world and the kinds of work available. It also helps you obtain more "hard skills," which will be useful in writing your resume.

- ☼ **Contacts and recommendations.** Internships give you contacts for future jobs and supervisors who can give you references and recommendations down the road.

☼ **Course credit/money.** Some internships offer small paychecks or stipends. Even if they don't, most do offer course credit.

☼ **"Negative experience."** There is a principle in art called "negative space"—drawing what is around your subject rather than the subject itself. Internships provide a similar platform for jobs—you can begin ruling out the work you don't like by trying it hands-on. It's much better to find this out now than later.

☼ **Jobs!** Often, internships themselves can become full-time jobs upon graduation, or lead to other positions in the company.

hot facts

In-turning Your Internship into a Job

According to a job search survey conducted in the Yahoo! HotJobs' College Community (http://community.hotjobs.com/hj-college), more than two-thirds (68 percent) of job seekers said that internships and work experience were most valuable in their search. One-fourth (26 percent) rated "major/GPA" as tops, and 6 percent touted extracurricular activities.

Even if you have graduated or are about to, it's not too late! You don't have to be a full-time student to get an internship. Contact your career counselor's office, even if you have already graduated, to see what opportunities you might qualify for. And if none are available right now, let the counselor know you would like to be considered the following semester. The staff may have to give priority to current students, but at least your name will be on the list!

WORK-STUDY

You are probably already familiar with work-study programs—opportunities to work on campus for several hours a week to earn money toward your tuition.

While you may not think doing the basketball team's laundry is a true, real-world work environment, it's still work experience. And some work-study jobs can be especially relevant: Accounting students can work in the bursar's office, library science majors can work in the library, marketing and merchandising majors in the bookstore, IT students in the computer lab, and so forth. For example, one job seeker, Sean, entered college as a drama major because he loved acting,

Outside the Box

You're Never Too Old for an Internship!

Internships aren't just available to denizens of the dormitory. Although traditionally intended for college students, anyone can apply to most internships—just be aware that you may receive little or no pay. You also need the right attitude—the most desirable candidates are eager to learn and do not mind taking direction from others. Internships, after all, are designed for people with little or no experience. But those who do take the chance to get a foot in the door of their dream career usually find that it's worth it.

For example, after college Elise accepted a regional sales position for a clothing company. She quickly became unhappy at her job and really wanted to be a journalist. She wasn't a student anymore, but she applied for a sports information/media relations internship in a large university's athletics department. Elise had to work a second job because she was only given a small yearly stipend. She had to travel constantly by bus to small towns, work nights and weekends, and was older than her fellow interns, who were all still students. But the contacts she made and the experience she gained proved invaluable in eventually getting her where she wanted to be.

but when he began his work-study job as a university theater ticket manager, he realized that he had solid business skills that could be used behind the scenes. He went on to manage the venue while receiving his master's degree in theater. Ultimately, he became the manager of that same university's auditorium/concert hall, as well as two other event facilities on campus.

Also, many students perform work-study jobs in close connection with professors, who can later be great references.

STUDY ABROAD

Study-abroad programs can be real feathers in the cap. They demonstrate an adventurous spirit, maturity, and—in many cases—the ability to manage a tight budget!

More important, studying abroad helps you develop the understanding that there is a big world out there beyond your college campus, with different people, economies, cultures, and customs. And of course, studying abroad is a chance to learn other languages—a very important skill in today's business world.

hot facts

Getting "In" with Top Internships

You never know where an internship might take you. Oprah Winfrey, Donald Trump, Katie Couric, and Ronald Reagan all were interns. For a stellar start to your career, try to land a gig with one of the thirty best internship programs in the U.S. (according to the Princeton Review's *Internship Bible* and *The Best 109 Internships*, *Peterson's Internships*, and the *Vault Guide to Top Internships*). These internships may lead to great jobs, pay well, or offer solid learning experiences and valuable contacts:

Academy of Television Arts
  and Sciences
American Cancer Society
Atlantic Records
Breakthrough Collaborative
CNN
CIA
Common Cause
Coors
Dallas Cowboys
Electronic Arts
FBI
Hill and Knowlton Public Relations
INROADS Minority Youth
  Scholarships
Kennedy Center

Lucasfilms
Marvel Comics
MTV
NASA
Nike
Northwestern Mutual
Procter & Gamble
Random House
San Diego Zoo
U.S. Olympic Committee
U.S. Supreme Court
Universal Studios
Volkswagen
Wall Street Journal
WGBH (Boston Public Television)
White House

Also keep in mind that even brief travel with family, youth groups, camps, or other organizations can be grounds for developing knowledge in languages and other cultures. Your family's cruise to the Bahamas probably wouldn't count, but a trip to build houses in Haiti is worth discussing on a resume (see more on "Volunteering" on page 40).

JOB FAIRS

Job fairs are large gatherings of companies' representatives for the purpose of getting to know you and explaining their current or pending job openings.

On-campus job fairs are often only open to students of that institution. But other public job fairs are open to any and all job seekers. The jobs available at job fairs tend to be junior or entry-level positions. (If you're an older job seeker, don't be intimidated if you're surrounded by college students and recent grads at a job fair. Your age and life experience can be what sets you apart in recruiters' minds.)

Job fairs are a fantastic way to find out about available jobs and practice your interviewing skills. Because you only get a couple of minutes with each company's recruiter, you are forced to hone your personal "**elevator speech**" (or "elevator pitch"), a business term for concisely describing your high points and skills in less than a minute—as if you were fortunate enough to share an elevator ride with the hiring manager.

▶**Action Item:** Elevator Speech

Write down a paragraph describing yourself and what you are looking for in a job. Include your skills and what you have to offer a company.

Now hone your speech until you can convey in roughly thirty to sixty seconds how great an asset you would be. For example:

> *"My name is Joe Job Seeker, and I am a writer seeking to create outstanding copy for an advertising firm in Minneapolis. I believe my skills would be best utilized in technology-related campaigns, but as a recent college graduate I realize I have a lot to learn and would be happy to start in this field in any capacity. I have a degree in English from the University of Chicago. While in school, I sold ads for the school newspaper and worked as coeditor of the literary magazine. I am a solid communicator, very deadline-oriented, and have training in Web design."*

You might not get a chance to recite your speech to a potential employer (and certainly don't launch into it like a job-seeking robot), but it helps you collect your thoughts before you interview.

Some career fairs are general, and feature all types of jobs. Others are for a specific field, such as teaching, and diversity fairs are becoming increasingly popular. Go to as many as you can, even if they don't focus on a field you are certain about, because there will still be a variety of jobs available. One job seeker went to a parochial school teaching job fair, and while she did not find the middle school English job she was hoping for, she did find a position as a librarian in an elementary school. Not only did she get to surround herself with books every day and teach students the value of reading and writing, but the parish offered to help pay for the remainder of her master's degree in education!

From the Desk of

Bob Toll
Chairman and CEO, Toll Brothers

As college graduates approach the job market, I would advise them to make certain that they are happy, intrigued, and almost consumed by the job they choose. If time doesn't pass quickly during the workday, then they are in the wrong job. If they have more time than they need, then they are in the wrong profession.

Probably the best career advice I ever received was from my law school days, when I learned that Socrates said: "It is a wise man who knows what he doesn't know." As for the smartest career choice I ever made, it was going into the homebuilding business. I have never been bored, not even for a second. The best job I ever had is the one I have now—building and running America's leading luxury homebuilding company. What was the worst career choice I ever made? Practicing law . . . but I recovered by quitting.

My first "real" job was working for a real estate agency, which I got through my father's recommendation. If I knew in my late teens and early twenties what I know now, I would have followed the traditional advice of going into investment real estate instead of real estate for sale. But then I don't think I would have enjoyed [my career] as much as I have.·

My advice for promoting yourself to employers: Work hard, come in early, and leave late. Try and handle as much as you think the person above you would permit.

Also, don't rule out "boring" jobs and companies. You never know—a local accounting firm might have a great entry-level assistant publications manager position available. A carpeting business might need a Web designer. Also, keep in mind that you may not be able to find your dream job or career right out of school anyway. As with internships, the goal right now is to get experience.

A few other things to keep in mind about job fairs: They are almost always free and they are frequent. You can find out about them through your local university career office, in newspapers, or on TV and radio.

take a memo

Fair Thee Well

Here are some practical tips for preparing for a job fair:

☼ Job fairs usually list the companies that will be attending. Research these ahead of time.

☼ Practice your greeting and your elevator speech in the mirror beforehand.

☼ Dress professionally.

☼ Bring more resumes than you think you will need.

Finally, when you're at the fair, try this handy tip: To "warm up," first go to a couple of booths you are fairly certain you are uninterested in. Practice with those recruiters before you move on to the jobs you'd really like. This will help you calm your nerves and get your skills to the forefront of your mind.

ALUMNI NETWORKS

Once you graduate, you almost have no excuse for not knowing about your college's alumni network—believe us, they will find you. Schools need donations and good word of mouth to thrive; they are always eager to keep in touch with their graduates.

Alumni are usually glad to help out new graduates. After all, you have something in common. You walked the same campus, cheered for the same football team, maybe even had the same crotchety economics professor. The topics for conversation starters are endless—and it's hard for someone to say "no" to a new grad who needs help.

And, of course, an alum might even be able to hire you. A graduate of your school from twenty years ago might run his own accounting firm now; another may be an executive with a sporting goods company; and another might be trying to launch a start-up or a really cool nonprofit and need help.

So join the alumni database, fill out the questionnaires the alumni office sends you, attend the alumni events in your town. No events? Ask the alumni office for contact information for alums in your area and call them for informational interviews (see page 41). Many schools even have formal programs that are specifically intended to help new grads connect with alumni in their fields.

take a memo

Volunteer for Success

We have many volunteers who come to us to keep busy and feel productive while they are in the midst of a job hunt. One of the things I have noticed is that volunteering, in addition to providing very rewarding experiences during "downtime," helps job hunters expand their networks by exposing them to people they would not ordinarily interact with. I have seen friendships develop among our volunteers and job opportunities develop as a result. This is actually something that we teach our clients (low-income women from the Washington, DC area). Not only is volunteer experience something to include on your resume, but you never know where it may lead you.

—Mary-Frances Wain, Executive Director, Suited for Change

VOLUNTEERING

The bad news about volunteering is that it won't make you any money—you'll have to find other resources in the meantime.

But, the good news is, these "jobs" are sure things! Volunteer organizations are always seeking help. True, some you approach may not have the type of volunteer work you want to do, but just keep trying and you'll find something. There are volunteer groups (nonprofits, houses of worship, hospitals, schools, animal rescue organizations, and the like) for just about anything you can imagine.

Another great thing to keep in mind is that volunteer organizations need the *same skills* a workplace would—computer skills, customer service, organization, event planning—the list goes on and on. Just because you're not being paid doesn't mean you're not learning valuable work skills. In fact, volunteering is a fantastic learning experience because you often have more freedom to make mistakes and ask questions than in a paying situation. You are demonstrating your commitment to the cause and your own career by using your free time to learn skills that help your community.

For example, if you help run a local soup kitchen, you're garnering skills for your resume such as supply management, public relations, customer service, crisis management, accounting, and more. Any employer would be happy to find this combination of skills—and the fact that you took it upon yourself to learn them makes you that much more of a valuable hire.

INFORMATIONAL INTERVIEWS

Informational interviews—informal conversations with those experienced in particular fields—are one of the least-utilized "golden opportunities." Entry-level job seekers tend to trust their parents, professors, or peers rather than going straight to the source to ask questions.

Informational interviews can be one of the best ways for a new college graduate or other job seeker to learn about jobs. And for once, *you* get to do the interviewing!

Perhaps *informational interview* sounds intimidating, but remember, working adults have a hard time saying "no" to a graduate—especially if they have college-age kids of their own! And you don't have to meet with a company president. Someone closer to a position similar to one you would hold might be more approachable for you and better able to give you information that relates to that job and field as you would experience it.

Informational interviews also give you a chance to practice your interviewing skills in a more relaxed environment. Yes, you should still dress professionally, and yes, you should still come prepared with smart questions and your relevant skills and experience in the forefront of your mind—and even bring a resume or two (but offer it only with the polite request that your interview subject "place it on file for future consideration"). Because there is not a job on the line, this is your chance to ask the big questions about the job and about how your skills might or might not fit into it, and get real answers from someone who knows.

(And while we can't promise anything, remember that job and internship offers do sometimes come from informational interviews. That is not their intended purpose, but it certainly is possible!)

▶**Action Items:** Make a list of three people/companies you would like to interview, and proceed to contact them about informational interviews.

1._____

     Phone number (   )_____ - _____

     E-mail _____

2._____

     Phone number (   )_____ - _____

     E-mail _____

3._____

　　　Phone number (　　)_____ - _____
　　　E-mail _____

While you wait for answers, prepare for the interviews by:

☼ Reading about the field and the company

☼ Noting why your interests and skills have drawn you toward this field

☼ Making a list of questions, such as:

- What is a typical day like?

- What types of degrees do you hold, and have they helped you in this field?

- What is the most important skill I need for a job in this field?

- How else would you recommend I bolster my skills for a job in this field?

Recommended Books

The Princeton Review Best 109 Internships by Mark Oldman & Samer Hamadeh (Random House Information Group, ISBN 0375763198, $21.00).

The Internship Bible, 2005 Edition by Mark Oldman & Samer Hamadeh (Random House Information Group, ISBN 0375764682, $25.00).

Scoring a Great Internship (Students Helping Students Series) by Ellen Rubinstein (Natavi Guides, ISBN 0971939284, $6.95).

Internships 2005: Find the Right Internship for You by the Staff of Peterson's Publishing (Thomson Learning, ISBN 0768914981, $26.95).

The Insider's Guide to Political Internships: What to Do Once You're in the Door by Grant Reeher & Mack Mariani (Westview Press, ISBN 0813340160, $17.00).

Gardner's Guide to Internships in New Media 2004: Computer Graphics, Animation, Multimedia by Garth Gardner & Marilyn Webber (Garth Gardner Company, ISBN 1589650085, $34.95).

Vault Guide to Top Internships (Vault Career Library Series) by Samer Hamadeh, Marcy Lerner & Mark Oldman (Vault, Inc., ISBN 1581312911, $14.95).

Recommended Web Sites

Yahoo! HotJobs—Finding a Job:
http://hotjobs.yahoo.com/findingajob

Association for International Practical Training:
www.aipt.org

BUNAC (British Universities North American Club)—
Offers a range of working holidays:
www.bunac.org

CDS International (Carl Duisberg Gesellschaft/Carl Duisberg Society)—
Offers Americans internships in Germany:
www.cdsintl.org

Council on International Educational Exchange (CIEE):
www.ciee.org

International Volunteer Programs Association:
www.volunteerinternational.org

CHAPTER 4

Navigating Rough Seas: Overcoming Job Search Obstacles

"English lit—how about you?"

What job requires forty hours a week, a professional wardrobe, complete commitment, 24/7 availability, has no benefits, and an annual salary of $0? Your job search.

Okay, it's not quite *that* bad, but in order for it to be successful, you have to start thinking of your job search as a full-time job.

Unfortunately, a few things stand in your way—distractions, money, living arrangements, pressure from family and friends, and your own hopes and expectations for your job. Of course, there is the biggest obstacle of all—your lack of experience as a job seeker! However, there is hope. Let's take a look at some of your obstacles and how you can overcome them.

INEXPERIENCE WITH THE JOB-SEEKING PROCESS

Remember the first time you dove into a pool, how frightening it was? Worrying about going into the water *upside down*, hitting the bottom, or getting water up your nose? You knew in your head that you could do it, but actually executing a dive was a different story because you'd never done it before.

Then do you remember the elation you felt when you accomplished it? Once you dove in, you could do it again and again. Sure there were some belly flops, but you learned from your mistakes as you went along and kept going.

It's human nature to fear the unknown. When you've never searched for a "real" job before, you may worry not just about whether you'll find a job, but also about the search itself. *How will I pay the rent? What can I do with an art history degree? What if I get stuck here in Anytown?* You could go on and on with your doubts.

Or you could put that energy into your job search. You don't have to let these worries get in the way. The only way to find a job is to get out there and start looking. Sure, you'll make mistakes. Yes, there will be interviews where you feel stumped. No, recruiters aren't always going to call you back, even when they promise they will. This is all normal—so don't panic!

The best thing you can do to overcome the inexperience obstacle is to **get experienced at job seeking**. Keep going forward and learn as you go along. Learn from your network. Read books like this one. Get feedback from family and friends on your resume and interview style. Go on informational job interviews to gain experience and get comfortable with the process. Get informed about the job searching process and you will get a job. (Without water up the nose, either.)

MONEY

Oh, that pesky green stuff. The ink may have barely dried on your degree and already you need cash.

Not only might you now be responsible for the first time for things such as food, bills, and rent, but the job searching process costs money too: You need good interview attire, an Internet connection, office supplies, cab fare, and the like. Sure you can write off some of it on your taxes—*next year!*—but how does that help you now? The old term for where you are is "salad days"—when money was tight and people lived on cheap food. Today the term might be "ramen days" or "pizza days." And, much as the term implies, you will have to be adept with your budgeting (such as relying on bulk foods) to get by.

You can find a roommate or roommates to save on rent. Groups of four or more can even rent entire houses—giving you the space of a house while cutting down on the rent. (Just be sure your housemates understand that you need quiet time to search for jobs.) You can also share bills and food expenses if you so choose.

Or, there's always the old-fashioned solution: Move back in with Mom and Dad (assuming they haven't thrown out your baseball card collection and turned your room into a gym). It may not be fun, but at least it's a roof over your head. And hey, that will motivate you to search harder. The sooner you find a job, the sooner you can get out of there!

hot facts

Can You Go Home Again?

Three-quarters (73 percent) of college students said they would move in with their parents after graduation to save money, in a survey taken in Yahoo! HotJobs' College Community (http://community.hotjobs.com/hj-college). What they didn't say: whether their parents would actually take them back.

Also, there is nothing wrong with taking a part-time job. It gives you money, skills, networking opportunities, and time to look for full-time jobs.

You can also consider "temping"—working part-time for different businesses, doing a variety of jobs (usually basic office type stuff, although it could be higher level) for short periods of time. You can sign on with "temp agencies," who give you assignments and handle your payments and benefits. Temping allows you to do a range of jobs, meet many different supervisors, and see a number of work environments. You can find contact information for local temp agencies in your phone book or online.

Student Loans

Never has a phrase instilled such fear into a new college graduate. Fortunately, with the help of your parents and an understanding bank, you can find a way to lower your monthly payment, interest rate, or defer payment altogether. Most loans do offer a grace period of several months after you graduate. Visit Salliemae.com (the nation's leading provider of higher education funding) for more information.

Be mindful, too, of taking on more debt. If you haven't already, you will soon begin receiving a host of credit card offers from various banks. Be careful. If you already have a credit card or cards, use them only in emergencies and pay as much as you can on them each month. Don't take on more debt. According to Yahoo!Finance, the average American household has $8,400 in credit card debt!

▶▲◀
hot facts ●
▶▼◀
Worth Its Weight in Work

Is there value in a college education, even if it doesn't always pay off? Yes, according to job seekers surveyed in Yahoo! HotJobs' College Community (http://community.hotjobs.com/hj-college). Over two-thirds of job seekers (68 percent) said that they would pursue a college degree even if it wouldn't affect their earning potential. So think about that every time you make a payment on those student loans.

Distractions

Some of the most frustrating obstacles you'll face as you begin your job search have nothing to do with your job search at all! Instead they are the daily distractions that seem bent on keeping you from finding a job. Distractions can range from being without a car to working from home while your teenage brother blares his stereo to . . . oh, look, a bird!

Distractions will chip away at your time and your patience until you don't have the energy to look for work. Here are some of the worst offenders and ways to guard against them.

Environment

You need peace and quiet for your job search. Writing a resume requires concentration, and imagine trying to conduct a phone interview with the family dog barking in the background!

Find a quiet spot or time when you have the house to yourself to conduct your job search, or go to the local library. If you have a cell phone, you can take it to a quiet spot for business calls. Search for jobs while others are away at work or school, and if necessary, skip the family vacation this year and use the peace and quiet for your search.

Be sure family and roommates know that you need the computer/phone line/ DSL for job searching—set aside specific time when it's "yours" if you have to.

E-mail

Set up a separate e-mail account for your job search and open only that one during your search time. Don't give the address to friends and family and don't use it for anything else besides your job search, or you may find yourself overwhelmed by spam. It's way too easy to get sucked into an ongoing conversation or a stroll through your best friend's online photo album of his hike along the Appalachian Trail. Do those things later, after your job search is finished for the day.

Friends

Your roommates and friends can be distractions of their own—directly, by pressuring you to do things other than your job search, or indirectly, simply by . . . existing. It's tough to write a cover letter when there is an impromptu party going on in the living room. And who hasn't walked through a room where everyone else is watching a movie—and plopped down on the couch next to them rather than attending to business? Seems innocent enough at first, but one night can turn into two, and before you know it, an entire month has zipped by and you haven't so much as checked your job search e-mail.

During your life as a student you had someone to answer to—a professor, a teacher, your parents. After you graduate, no one is telling you what to do and it's wonderful. And risky. This time in your life is critical. You must learn to discipline yourself and stick to your job search structure, regardless of what your friends are doing. It's fine to party, if it's a reward for a hard day's work of job searching. Set goals for yourself each day (apply to five jobs, make three informational interview calls, etc.). But learn how to work first, have fun later.

THINK Outside the Box

When "Distractions" Are Your Life

"Avoiding distractions" is often easier said than done. If you're a parent, already employed, or have other major responsibilities, you can't always put them on hold to look for a job. What you can try to do is carve out some time for your search, no matter how little. Make a plan that details when you're going to work on your job search and for how long. Specify dates and times. Then set some goals, no matter how small, for that time.

For example, plan to spend one hour every other day on your search. Then devote certain days to searching online for jobs and other days to sending out resumes. You'll make progress one step at a time.

PRESSURE

Pressure comes at you both internally and externally during a job search. You, of course, probably feel pressure from within to find a job that you will love, that will give you freedom, money, and a chance to make your mark on the world. That's a lot to ask of a first job.

Meanwhile, your dad wonders aloud about the size of the bonus check your next-door neighbor (who is your age and had a lower GPA than you) received from her new pharmaceutical sales job. Your boyfriend of two years is quite happy in Anytown and prefers that you stay there as well. In the news you hear that the economy is up one day, down the next, and thousands are looking for work.

With pressure like that, who wouldn't want to give up and wait tables the rest of your life?

Hopefully you.

You cannot always control what you see and hear every day, and you cannot control others, but you can control your reactions to external events. Stay calm and remember that a career is a journey, not a destination.

You cannot enter this process and expect to score a bull's-eye on the first try. For now, don't worry about what the news says, or the jobs your friends find— focus only on your own job search, day by day—writing a great resume, making contacts, practicing your interview skills. Meanwhile, stay physically and mentally healthy—eat right, exercise, and pray or meditate if you feel so inclined.

Of course, the people who care about us the most want the best for us and want us around. But the fact is, this is your life. No one will have to get up every day and go into that office, or that studio, or that Antarctic research station but you. Down the road you can wind up resenting people you love if you feel they pressured you into making a decision you weren't happy with. Yes, you have other people to consider, but make sure the one you consider first is you. (If necessary, a psychological or career counselor can help you bolster your strength in making these decisions.)

Fear and Depression

A certain amount of malaise at this point in your life is to be expected. You do have some major changes and decisions to face. But if you find yourself losing sleep from worry, or are so anxious about job hunting (sweaty, can't eat, or eat too much) that you can't focus, you might want to seek outside help from family or a significant other, your doctor, your clergyperson, or a psychological counselor. They can help you prioritize your tasks and view your problems more objectively. (See the box below for some useful resources for coping with fear, stress, and depression.)

take a memo

Keeping Calm, Keeping Centered

Feeling overwhelmed, depressed, or sad about your job search? Here are some Web sites to help you locate valuable sources of assistance:

- National Board of Certified Counselors (NBCC) CounselorFind: www.nbcc.org/cfind
- National Hopeline Network: www.hopeline.com
- National Institute of Mental Health: Depression www.nimh.nih.gov/healthinformation/depressionmenu.cfm

You can also contact your university's counseling center or student development center for guidance.

DOUBTS AND DECISIONS

Some of the biggest obstacles you'll encounter are those you—or well-meaning others—place in your way. You've won half the job-hunting battle if you can learn now to be patient when these doubts and decisions plague you. The following are some of the most common ones and some tips to help you cope.

You've Gotten a Degree and You Still Have No idea What You Want to Do

Don't worry. Neither do thousands of other grads in your shoes. You will. But it takes time to figure it out, using methods we've explained like Web sites, informational interviews, and skills assessment. Eventually you will find yourself drawn in one, or maybe more, directions. In the meantime, finding a job—any job—for the experience is the key.

For example, Barbara was unsure about what she wanted to do, but she knew that she wanted to live in New York. Through on-campus recruiting, she accepted a sales position with a company in Manhattan; she hoped to support herself financially and gain practical work experience while considering her options. During her first year in New York, Barbara spoke to everyone she knew about his or her job, and she came to realize that she was most interested in film. After doing some research and a lot of networking, she left her sales job to work as a production assistant on a feature film—and she's happily working in film today.

I Want to Be a Doctor and a Lawyer and an Astronaut . . .

Maybe you feel yourself pulled in several, wildly different career directions. Again, don't worry. This is a good sign that you have healthy interests in a number of activities and that you can be happy in any of them. Just try to focus on one in particular *for now*.

Think of your career as a big tapestry. On one side, the threads are knotted and rough, but on the other side, every thread leads somewhere beautiful. You can't make a wrong choice.

You Expect the "Perfect Job" Right Out of College

First of all, a "perfect job" or "dream job" is a subjective thing that will change as you move through life. You need to have realistic expectations and be open to a range of opportunities and possibilities.

A career is a path consisting of various jobs and choices you make along the way. As you progress through your career, what you're looking for in a job will

From the Desk of

Brad Meltzer
New York Times Best-Selling Author

When I graduated from college, I had debt to pay off. I didn't come from a rich family. They wouldn't pay for me to take a year off and travel through France after school. It was a matter of hunting and storing my food in my cheeks. So I set my sights on law school.

But I knew a guy at a magazine, and he said, "Come work for me, and I'll teach you the business world. If you love it, stay—if not, you'll at least have some experience and some money." I moved to Boston to work for him. A week later he left the company. I was wrecked. I thought my life was over.

I decided what we all decide—to write a novel. I thought it was captivating and brilliant...and I quickly got twenty-four rejections. In fact, I had only sent the book to twenty publishers, so some of them actually rejected me twice!

But I learned that I loved writing. I loved talking to imaginary people. So I told myself, "If they don't like this one, I'll write another and another and another until I come up with one they do like."

Headlines can be depressing but there is no better way around a bad economy—around anything—than a creative solution. You just have to build a better mousetrap. We are a country of marketers. You have to figure out how to make yourself stand out from the thousands of other college graduates. Personally, I don't think anything matters more than creativity, but everyone has gifts they can use to make their niche.

After my twenty-fourth rejection I started writing *The Tenth Justice*. I can't possibly explain how I managed to do it, or why this particular book worked. When I look back, nearly twenty-four people had told me to give up. I'm not saying, "I'm right, they're wrong," but when I look back I see that life is subjective. We each have our own opinion. Whatever you do, don't let anyone tell you no. There is a place for you. The only way to find the dream is to chase it.

take a memo

From Rags to Riches

Many celebrities didn't start out that way. See if you can match the star to the job:

1. Elvis Presley	A. Lawyer
2. Marilyn Monroe	B. Truck Driver
3. Henri Matisse	C. Dunkin' Donuts clerk
4. Madonna	D. Hairdresser
5. Danny DeVito	E. Art professor
6. Whoopi Goldberg	F. Coffin polisher
7. Samuel Morse	G. Assembly line worker
8. Sean Connery	H. Funeral home makeup artist

(Answers: 1-B, 2-G, 3-A, 4-C, 5-D, 6-H, 7-E, 8-F)

change as you move, build a family, and make other life choices. Unless you decide to make crime your career, you really can't make a mistake from which you can't recover at this point.

So stop putting so much pressure on yourself. Focus on finding a job that will give you experience. For more introspection, refer back to the exercises you completed in chapter 1.

You Don't Know Where You Want to Live

No more are you bound by a college campus or your parents' house. You're dying to get away, but as the entire world stretches out before you, you don't know where to begin. Do you pick a city and look for a job, or pick a job and look for a city? How do you know you'll like Seattle? Is Chicago really that windy?

On the other hand, maybe you want to stay right where you are—which means you have to find a job there in Anytown, USA. But perhaps there are no advertising firms in Anytown, or the accounting firms there aren't hiring entry-level applicants. Now what?

Consider, too, the things that inspire you away from work. If kayaking and mountain climbing are your passions, then maybe Denver would appeal to you. Like the ocean? There are many cities and towns that can have you in a sky-scraper in the morning, and surfing by the afternoon.

▶ ▲ ◀
hot facts •
▶ ▼ ◀

Cities with the Most Jobs Posted on Yahoo! HotJobs:

1. New York, NY	18. Philadelphia, PA	35. Toronto, ONT
2. Chicago, IL	19. Indianapolis, IN	36. Richmond, VA
3. San Francisco, CA	20. Phoenix, AZ	37. Tucson, AZ
4. Denver, CO	21. Irvine, CA	38. Columbus, OH
5. San Jose, CA	22. Miami, FL	39. Pittsburgh, PA
6. Los Angeles, CA	23. Seattle, WA	40. Fremont, CA
7. San Diego, CA	24. Santa Clara, CA	41. Las Vegas, NV
8. Atlanta, GA	25. Tampa, FL	42. McLean, VA
9. Boston, MA	26. Pasadena, CA	43. Portland, OR
10. Salt Lake City, UT	27. Austin, TX	44. Jacksonville, FL
11. Dallas, TX	28. Minneapolis, MN	45. Scottsdale, AZ
12. Washington, DC	29. Baltimore, MD	46. Walnut Creek, CA
13. Sunnyvale, CA	30. Orlando, FL	47. Cleveland, OH
14. Houston, TX	31. Mountain View, CA	48. Milwaukee, WI
15. Sacramento, CA	32. Charlotte, NC	49. Hartford, CT
16. Oakland, CA	33. El Segundo, CA	50. Plano, TX
17. Cincinnati, OH	34. Detroit, MI	

But ultimately, **go where the jobs are**. A job, not geography, should be your biggest focus at this point. If you like where you are, begin your search there and then gradually expand your search until you find available jobs. Also keep in mind relocation costs. Some companies will help a lot, some a little, others not at all.

Choose without regret, knowing that wherever you go you will make friends, have fun, and learn new things.

Should I Go to Grad School?

Graduate school is a necessity for many careers (medicine, law, academics) and a good choice for others even if not necessary. Grad school can also be a comforting thought for graduates facing a tough job market, struggling with their job search or afraid of the "working world."

With grad school comes not only the same obstacles of money, living arrangements, and so on, but you'll also be continuing to add to your already growing loans for at least another year in most cases. Having an extra degree is

hot facts ●

Metro Areas: Get the "Big Picture"

Want to expand your job search? Instead of limiting your search to a city, focus on its metro area. A metro area includes a city and its communities, or suburbs. For example, the Washington, DC, metro area includes not just the city itself, but also nearby parts of Maryland and Virginia.

Most online job boards give you the option to search for jobs in a specific city only or to include jobs in its metro area. The metro areas with the most jobs posted on Yahoo! HotJobs are:

1. New York, Northern New Jersey, Long Island
2. San Francisco, Oakland, San Jose
3. Los Angeles, Riverside, Orange County
4. Chicago, Gary, Kenosha
5. Washington, Baltimore
6. Dallas, Fort Worth
7. Philadelphia, Wilmington, Atlantic City
8. Boston, Worcester, Lawrence
9. Atlanta
10. San Diego
11. Houston, Galveston, Brazoria
12. Miami, Fort Lauderdale
13. Seattle, Tacoma, Bremerton
14. Phoenix, Mesa
15. Denver, Boulder, Greeley
16. Sacramento, Yolo
17. Detroit, Ann Arbor, Flint
18. St. Louis
19. Tampa, St. Petersburg, Clearwater
20. Minneapolis, St. Paul
21. Jacksonville
22. Columbus
23. Indianapolis
24. San Antonio
25. Charlotte, Gastonia, Rock Hill
26. Raleigh, Durham, Chapel Hill
27. Cincinnati, Hamilton
28. Memphis
29. Las Vegas
30. West Palm Beach, Boca Raton
31. Milwaukee, Racine
32. Richmond, Petersburg
33. Rochester
34. Nashville
35. Hartford
36. Dayton, Springfield
37. Omaha
38. Birmingham
39. Tucson
40. Louisville

certainly a bonus on your resume, but is it really necessary? An additional degree may get you a higher starting salary—but it may also cause recruiters to dismiss you as "overqualified." Talk to people in the fields you are considering about their degrees, as well as professors in those programs, before you decide. Sometimes getting out into the working world and earning your degree from the "school of hard knocks" will serve you better.

For example, after graduating from an Ivy League school, Bill earned his master's in business administration at the prestigious Wharton School. He gave it his all—including case studies, internships, and study abroad. Meanwhile his undergrad classmates were already earning a paycheck while Bill was adding to his already six-figure debt. His only income came from his military reservist duties every other weekend. When he graduated, there was such a glut of highly qualified new consultants applying for the same jobs in New York, that he settled for a job in Chicago, away from his wife and new baby five days a week. The available jobs nearer his family either paid too little or ruled him out as "overqualified." He left after an unhappy year and went on active military duty while looking for a job closer to home. After two years as an officer, he was offered a high-ranking analyst's job with a government security agency—and decided to stay in the military until retirement. He hadn't planned on the military as a career, but loved where he ultimately ended up. And while his graduate degree was helpful, it wasn't what got him there.

▶**Action Items:** List the five things holding you back most. Then list five strategies for dealing with each one. Sometimes just writing your worries down on paper helps to diminish them and show you that these obstacles are surmountable. Once you acknowledge them, you'll be able to formulate a plan to deal with them.

1. Obstacle _____

   Strategy _____

2. Obstacle _____

   Strategy _____

3. Obstacle _____

   Strategy _____

4. Obstacle _____

   Strategy _____

5. Obstacle _____

   Strategy _____

Recommended Books

Graduate!: Everything You Need to Succeed after College by Kristin M. Gustafson (Capital Books, Inc., ISBN 1892123282, $14.95).

The Everything After College Book: Real-World Advice for Surviving and Thriving on Your Own by Leah Furman & Elina Furman (Adams Media Corporation, ISBN 1558508473, $14.95).

A Car, Some Cash, and a Place to Crash: The Only Post-College Survival Guide You'll Ever Need by Rebecca Knight (Rodale Press, Inc., ISBN 1579546269, $17.95).

A Man, a Can, a Plan: 50 Great Guy Meals Even You Can Make! by David Joachim (Rodale Press, Inc., ISBN 1579546072, $15.95).

Personal Budgeting (Barnes & Noble Basics Series) by Barbara Wagner (Silver Lining Books, ISBN 0760737193, $9.95).

Saving Money (Barnes & Noble Basics Series) by Barbara Loos (Silver Lining Books, ISBN 0760740208, $9.95).

Everything Personal Finance for the 20s and 30s: Erase Your Debt, Personalize Your Budget, and Plan Now to Secure Your Future by Debby Fowles (Adams Media, ISBN 1580629709, $14.95).

Take Control of Your Student Loan Debt by Robin Leonard & Deanne Loonin (Nolo, ISBN 0873377079, $26.95).

The Complete Idiot's Guide® to Managing Your Time by Jeff Davidson (Alpha, ISBN 0028642635, $16.95).

Recommended Web Sites

Yahoo! Finance:
http://finance.yahoo.com

Yahoo! Finance Planning Center:
http://planning.yahoo.com

The Motley Fool:
www.fool.com

SallieMae:
www.salliemae.com

CounselorFind:
www.nbcc.org/cfind

Managing Job Search Stress:
www.internationalcollege.edu/pdf/CC_stress.pdf

National Institute of Mental Health—Depression:
www.nimh.nih.gov/healthinformation/depressionmenu.cfm

CHAPTER 5

The World Wide *Employment* Web:
Taking Your Search Online

n chapter 3, we looked at some of the popular tools for finding a job—including some unique opportunities for current students and recent grads, such as college career centers and alumni networks. In addition, there are two other methods every contemporary job seeker should incorporate into his or her search: the **Internet** and **networking**. (We'll talk more about networking in chapter 6.)

The Internet has changed the entire landscape of job searching. Until a decade or so ago, job seekers could only search newspaper classifieds and send hard copies of their resumes and cover letters via "snail mail." Today, job sites like Yahoo! HotJobs allow you to search and apply for jobs faster and more efficiently than ever before.

In this chapter, we'll take a look at these advantages and how you can make the most of your online job search.

BENEFITS OF ONLINE JOB SITES

Speed isn't the only advantage job sites offer. With assistance like detailed job ads, e-mail search agents, company research, salary calculators, privacy tools, and much more, the Internet gives you every advantage in getting the job short of the hiring manager's home phone number! And, it's worth noting that sites like Yahoo! HotJobs make these tools available absolutely FREE to job seekers!

A successful job search requires the full spectrum of resources at your disposal. While you would never want to ignore traditional help wanted ads, newspapers, and job boards, make sure you use the full potential of Yahoo! Hotjobs' tools dedicated to finding you the right job.

Powerful Search Tools

One of the biggest innovations of the Internet is making information accessible— FAST! Online job sites take this general benefit and apply it to job openings.

Sites like Yahoo! HotJobs offer job seekers several different options for searching job openings. You can choose to search by keyword, location, company, salary, experience level, employer type (direct employer or staffing agency), or how recently the job was posted. And, when you find a search that works for you, you can save it so you can refer back to it later. Compare those options with your local newspaper!

Collected Job Listings

Recently Yahoo! HotJobs put its cutting-edge technology to work to "scrape" jobs from all over the Internet. In other words, no more searching dozens of sites

THINK Outside the Box

The Hidden Job Market

The Society for Human Resources Management (SHRM), as well as many other career industry authorities, estimates that some 60–80 percent of jobs are filled not by job ads or the Internet, but by word-of-mouth and connections.

In other words, they are part of the "hidden" job market. These are jobs that may never even be publicly posted. Advertising jobs can be expensive for companies, so often they will announce a job internally and by word-of-mouth first. Sometimes companies will even offer cash bonuses to employees to help fill certain positions.

The hidden job market is one you'll do well to investigate, even now at the beginning point of your career. You can tap into it through your network (letting friends and contacts know you are seeking work) and by following company trends (if you see in the newspaper that a company plans to launch a big new product, there's a good chance that company will be hiring, even if no jobs are formally posted).

Another approach is to use your internship work or temporary work to get "into" a company, where you can watch bulletin boards and listen to water-cooler banter for upcoming jobs—long before the general public is privy to this information.

to find the job you want: Instead, enter your search terms to select from a comprehensive collection of sites from across the Web.

Detailed Job Ads

Online job ads are the best thing to happen to job seekers in decades. Why? Because they contain tons more information than their print predecessors, including the criteria recruiters and hiring managers use to evaluate candidates.

Stop and think about that for a second. Online job ads are like having the teacher's key to the chemistry final! But using the job ad is not cheating at all, because the hiring manager and recruiter want you to have the information. They pay for you to have the information. So, it's really more like an open-book exam, with the book provided by the teacher!

So how much more information are we talking about? Well, here's a typical newspaper job ad:

X-RAY MRI TECHNOLOGIST
ARRT registered. F/T & P/T. Good sa-
lary & bfts, Upper Eastside pvt radiolo-
*gy practice. Fax 212-***-*****

Newspapers charge employers per word or per line to print their job ads. So, employers pinch pennies by pinching words. The result, as you can see, looks more like a telegraph than a job ad.

Enter online job boards and job ads start to look altogether different. Here's an ad for a similar job:

MRI Technologist
Job ID: MRI
Location: Boston, MA
Date Posted: 12/1/2005

MRI Technologist

The Opportunity
The opportunities are endless at ABC Imaging Company. We employ over 15,000 people at 9 U.S. and 2 international locations

We offer full-time and part-time positions as well as a flexible work schedule. Plus, qualified candidates may be eligible for signing bonuses and relocation reimbursement!

The Company
ABC Imaging Company is a leading U.S. health care provider. Our diagnostic services including magnetic resonance imaging (MRI), single photon emission computed tomography (SPECT), ultrasound and positron emission tomography (PET).

Located in the heart of Boston, MA, we provide first-rate care for patients and first-rate opportunities for health care professionals. Get access to the most advanced health care technologies and enjoy a generous benefits program.

The Job Description
Perform patient imaging procedures and patient safety protocols. Handle diverse patients (outpatient, ER and in-house) and cover calls on a rotating basis. Position patients on the examining table, enter patient data into data-base and perform high-quality images. Transfer patients to and from gurneys in an acute, busy health care setting.

The Job Requirements
Graduation from an accredited two-year program in Radiologic Technology. One year of related experience and/or training. American Registry of Radiologic Technologist (ARRT) certification preferred as well as applicable state license. Certification according to ACR guidelines.

Contact Us
Jane Doe, Recruiter
janed@abcimagingcompany.com
fax 123-456-7890
www.abcimagingcompany.com

ABC Imaging Company is an affirmative action/equal opportunity M/F/D/V employer.

| Apply to Job |

The major online job boards do not charge companies based on the length of their ads. Therefore, companies include more information in their ads. This additional information allows job seekers to more effectively tailor their resumes and cover letters to job openings.

take a memo

Standard Components of an Online Job Ad

Most online job ads will contain some or all of the following:

General Company Information: Provides some background on the company, including its location, type of business, benefits, and number of employees. This is where the company attempts to "sell" itself to job seekers.

General Job Description: Paints a portrait of the job in broad strokes, including an overview of responsibilities and how the position fits into the organization.

Responsibilities: Runs down the list of day-to-day duties associated with the job.

Requirements: Includes experience level, education, and familiarity with certain tools, procedures, or software programs. This section may also include "soft skills," such as being "deadline-driven" or "detail-oriented."

How to Apply: Gives applicants specific instructions including pre-ferred resume format and whether or not to include additional information such as a job reference code or salary requirements.

A Central Location for All Your Materials

One of the frustrating aspects of conducting a job search is keeping up with what you sent to whom and when. Job Web sites alleviate that burden by giving you one repository for all of your job search "stuff." They allow you to store multiple versions of your resume and cover letter, remind you what dates you applied to which positions, and also provide statistics on how often your resume is being viewed by hiring companies—if you have posted your resume and chosen to make it accessible.

Resume Database

Online job sites allow you to turn the tables a bit on recruiters. Instead of just helping you looking for jobs and trying to get onto the recruiters' radar screens, job sites let you post your own personal online billboard—and the recruiters can come to you. Worried about your current boss spotting your resume online? Job sites like Yahoo! HotJobs feature privacy settings that allow you to block specified companies from viewing your resume (see page 65 for more on the subject of online privacy).

Online Communities

Online message boards allow you to "meet" other job seekers (not to mention the occasional recruiter on the hunt for talent!) and get their thoughts on jobs and companies. Just remember that some users may have a score to settle with a company that laid them off, so don't believe everything you read.

Research Resource

With e-mail newsletters, articles, and resources for career counseling and resume writing, job Web sites are bastions of career advice.

Industry news feeds help you keep up with the latest stories and trends in your area of interest—very helpful when you're writing a cover letter and need a solid statistic to throw in or when you're preparing for an interview and want to appear knowledgeable about recent industry developments.

E-mail newsletters keep you abreast of important information in your chosen industry when you don't have time to do your own research. They often include the latest industry news, topical community posts and polls, as well as lists of companies that are currently hiring. Yahoo! HotJobs offers newsletters covering finance, government, health care, human resources, technology, and sales. And, just in case you're interested, HotJobs has a newsletter especially written for recent college graduates. You can sign up for this or any of HotJobs' other newsletters at: www.hotjobs.com/newsletters.

take a memo

Avoiding Job Scams

They say that if something is "too good to be true," it probably is. This is definitely the case for some of the job postings and messages you'll see online, in the newspaper, on coffee shop bulletin boards, or elsewhere—for example, "WORK AT HOME!! MAKE $$$!!"

While some offers are legitimate, you should beware of job scams—like "phishing," for example. Phishing scams involve a con artist posing as a real business to obtain your personal or financial information. Here's how you can avoid this and other scams:

Don't offer any financial information. Ever. No recruiter would ever need your bank account number or credit card number. Sometimes sensitive information like your Social Security number will be requested during an in-person interview, but **never** over the phone.

Don't offer any money either. Ever. Work-at-home scams are notorious for this—asking for money upfront for "materials" or guaranteeing fast, easy success. Not true. Starting a home-based business is a noble idea, but it requires time and persistence. Use your common sense—there is no true "get rich quick" job.

Understand and use privacy features. Check Web sites' privacy policies, and if a recruiter calls you, be sure to check to make sure she is legit (try the Better Business Bureau, www.bbb.org).

Scammed? If you feel you have been targeted in a scam, contact your bank and credit card companies right away. You should also contact a credit reporting agency, such as Equifax (www.equifax.com) as well as the Better Business Bureau and the Internet Fraud Complaint Center (www.ifccfbi.gov/index.asp).

Salary tools help you calculate what you are "worth" in the marketplace. Find out what a certain job should pay and how that varies by region. This tool is extremely helpful when you're going into a negotiation or considering relocation.

For Your (and Potential Employers') Eyes Only

Everyone is concerned about the privacy of his or her career information. You don't want a complete stranger to stumble across your resume and see your contact information, and you don't want just any old employer to be able to see it either—certainly not your boss if you happen to be currently employed. With job Web sites, you can choose to make your resume public—meaning it will be searchable by the employers and staffing agencies that pay to use the site—or private—meaning your resume is not searchable and can only be shared when you physically send it to a hiring company.

In addition to these options, some sites give you the option of blocking certain employers from viewing your resume—regardless of whether the resume is public or private. Yahoo! HotJobs pioneered this feature, which it calls "HotBlock." You simply enter the names of the companies you do not want to be able to view your resume, and recruiters who identify themselves with that company will not be shown your resume in their search results. It's an ideal way to help keep your current boss from finding out about your job search.

E-mail Search Agents

Truly one of the most fantastic tools of job Web sites is the e-mail search agent. These powerful tools use your preferred search criteria to scan new job postings as they are added to the site. When a match is found, you're alerted by e-mail. Most sites allow you to choose the frequency of the alerts (daily, weekly, and so forth), and offer you the ability to refine your search criteria at any time.

START YOUR (SEARCH) ENGINES!

Now that we've introduced some of the innovations job sites offer you as a job seeker, you may be wondering, *How do I get started?*

For most sites, posting your resume is the first step.

Posting Your Resume

You can submit your resume in several ways, depending on the site:

- ☼ Create a resume by filling in set fields
- ☼ Cut and paste the resume from a document
- ☼ Upload it directly to the site's database from your computer

Note that when you cut and paste you'll need to use ASCII (American Standard Code for Information Exchange), a universal font that any computer can read (also known as "plain text"). Here's a tip: You'll want to save a copy of your ASCII resume both with the job Web site and on your own hard drive—so

take a memo

Plain Text Tips

While plain text resumes may seem boring, their simplicity allows recruiters to view them regardless of the software they use.

Tools: Use a text editor such as Notepad to write the resume. If you don't have, or can't find your text editor, you can download NoteTab Light here for free: www.download.com/3000-2352-10008280.html

Creating the resume: If you're writing the resume from scratch, keep the organization clean and simple. If you cut and paste a formatted resume, you'll notice much of the formatting will be lost. Your font will be uniform and any text with bold or italics will be replaced with plain text. Save the resume as a text document (with a ".txt" extension).

Spell-check: A text editor likely won't have a spell-check function, so perform that in your word processing program, and then resave the updated plain text resume in the text editor.

E-mail: If you are requested to submit a resume pasted directly into an e-mail, some e-mail programs will add formatting you don't want. Double-check your characters and spacing, and be sure your e-mail program's features such as "Rich Text Editor" are turned off.

Formatting: Use all CAPS to make headers stand out from body text. Use asterisks or dashes as "bullets." Avoid the "Tab" key; instead use the space bar. Finally, always e-mail a copy of your plain-text resume to yourself before sending it to a recruiter. This gives you a chance to see the resume as the recruiter will see it.

when you need to enter the resume into another Web site, you'll already have an ASCII copy to cut and paste. (See chapter 8 for more on resumes.)

Along with a resume you'll need to store a basic version of your cover letter. However, you'll want to personalize it as much as you can and customize it to the job when you apply—don't just write a generic letter and send it to every opportunity. Take the time to use the site's "Edit" function to edit and save a version appropriate to the job you are applying for. (We'll discuss cover letters in chapter 7.)

Finally, as you upload your documents, remember to edit and proofread them before you begin submitting them for jobs.

Find the Right One: Searching for Jobs Online

Most job Web sites have both "quick search" (keywords, job category, and location) as well as "advanced search" (keywords, multiple job categories and locations, salary requirements, full-time or part-time, etc.) functions. Quick searches give you a broader idea of what is available; advanced searches help you narrow your focus.

As an entry-level job seeker, we recommend that you start with a broader search—don't make your criteria so narrow that you miss out on opportunities. For example, if you are uncertain what you want as a job, you might want to just search by location or industry to see what you find. Once you have an idea, use additional keywords to help you hone your search.

Also, be aware that your interest could span any number of jobs and industries. For example, if you're interested in writing, look at banking, marketing, journalism, public relations—any field that requires communication (and that's pretty much any field!). So don't limit yourself.

Finally don't rule out relocating just yet. A great job for you may be waiting a thousand miles away. See what's out there before you make up your mind where you want to be.

▶ ▲ ◀
hot facts •
▶ ▼ ◀
Who's Hiring

Here's a list of the hottest industries, based on the number of jobs posted on Yahoo! HotJobs in 2005.

1. Sales	14. Restaurant/Food Service
2. Accounting/Finance	15. Telecommunications
3. Technology	16. Human Resources
4. Health Care	17. Customer Service
5. Engineering/Architecture	18. Advertising/Public Relations
6. Retail	19. Legal
7. Banking/Mortgage	20. Construction/Facilities
8. Insurance	21. Management Consulting
9. Marketing	22. Real Estate
10. Pharmaceutical/Biotech	23. Hospitality/Travel
11. Internet/New Media	24. Transportation/Logistics
12. Manufacturing/Operations	25. Education/Training
13. Clerical/Administrative	

Once you've entered your criteria, you'll get a list of available jobs. Click on the ones that appeal to you (maybe even the ones that don't sound so appealing—at first!) and study the job ads in detail for hints on duties, culture, keywords to help you tailor your search, and compensation as well as what you'll need to submit, and to whom. Use this information to compose a customized cover letter and resume, then apply!

OTHER ONLINE RESOURCES

In addition to the major job Web sites, there are also other Web sites you can utilize in your search:

Ooooh, the OOH!

If you have a question about pretty much any job in the U.S. today, the Department of Labor (DOL) and its *Occupational Outlook Handbook* (in book form or at http://stats.bls.gov/oco/home.htm) will most likely offer detailed information on it.

For more than 270 types of jobs, the OOH details everything from working conditions to required education to salary to statistics. (Did you know that more than five out of ten fishermen were self-employed last year?) Revised every two years, it also projects what fields will grow or decline throughout the upcoming years. Use the OOH to get a basic idea of what your chosen fields will be like and to learn about the "downsides." (Remember fishing? It's also one of the country's most dangerous occupations.)

Industry/Trade Organization Web sites

Perhaps you know the industry you like, but are not sure about which companies to work for or what kind of opportunities there are in the field. Use industry or trade organization events and Web sites to find the answers.

"Industries" are specific branches of manufacturing and trade—health care, technology, finance, and the like. "Trade organizations" are groups within those industries that represent people in a certain occupation—nursing, Web development, journalism, and so on.

For example, journalism trade organization members may write for newspapers, radio, or science fiction magazines. Yet any writer can benefit from groups like the Society of Professional Journalists (www.spj.org) and Writers Guild of America, west (www.wga.org), provided he or she meets membership requirements. Trade organizations like these represent writers as a whole and foster learning, networking, benefits, and, of course, job searching.

By joining these groups and communicating online, you can be the first to find out about job openings and develop relationships with people who might have good leads on work. (If you can join and attend group meetings in person, so much the better—the networking opportunities are superb. Some have "student" membership prices. If dues are too expensive, you might try finding a free group in your local community for marketing professionals, women in technology, photographers, and so on.)

take a memo

A Sampling of Industry/Trade Organization Sites:
American Bankers Association: www.aba.com/default.htm
American Bar Association: www.abalawinfo.com
American Hospital Association: www.aha.org/aha/index.jsp
American Insurance Association: www.aiadc.org
American Nurses Association: www.nursingworld.org
American Psychological Association: www.apa.org
Cellular Telecommunications Industry Association: www.ctia.org
Collegiate Sports Information Directors of America: www.cosida.com
International Game Developers Association: www.igda.org
National Education Association: www.nea.org
National Press Photographers Association: www.nppa.org
Software Developers Association: www.sdasc.org

The Horse's Mouth: Company Web Sites

Today most companies have Web sites with sections for employment, and often their own databases to which you can submit a resume.

What makes company Web sites particularly valuable, though, is that you can begin to learn about their culture—their dress, communication style, working hours. Most company Web sites are upfront about their culture and benefits because they want to attract employees who will make a good fit. By reading press releases, annual reports, and executive bios, you can get further insight into their mission, products, and services—and expectations of employees.

Also, once you decide to apply for a job at a certain company, you can use the Web site information to tailor your cover letter with the correct contact information and tone.

Diversity Web Sites

Sites such as the Hispanic Alliance for Career Enhancement (www.HACE-USA.org), the Black Collegian Online (www.black-collegian.com), and Career Women (www.careerwomen.com) help minorities find potential jobs and become familiar with their employment rights.

Newspapers and Trade Magazines

Unfortunately, applying to jobs listed in paper publications moves a little slowly. By the time you circle an ad, the recruiter may have received a dozen other resumes from online job seekers. Nor do you get a full understanding of the job from a print ad. Fortunately, many larger newspapers and trade magazines have Web sites in which the same—and even additional—jobs are listed.

However, newspapers and magazines are portable—great for sneaking a peek on the train or over breakfast. And it's always good to read these publications for industry news—a trade magazine will have an article on possible acquisitions at a company (thus more potential jobs), whereas the company's Web site will not.

FROM THE NET TO NETWORKING

The Internet is the fastest, easiest way to launch a full-scale job search, one that can continue even after you've turned your computer off and gone to bed.

However, there is one more tool you'll need to use as you search for jobs—networking. In chapter 6 we'll discuss networking—how to capitalize on the network you already have, to expand it, and to use it to find a great job!

Recommended Books

Occupational Outlook Handbook 2004–2005, U.S. Department of Labor (JIST Works, Inc., ISBN 1563709880, $16.90).

Everything Online Job Search Book: Find the Jobs, Send Your Resume and Land the Career of Your Dreams—All Online! by Steven Graber & Barry Littman (Adams Media Corporation, ISBN 1580623654, $12.95).

Guide to Internet Job Searching 2004–2005 by Margaret Riley Dikel & Frances E. Roehm (The McGraw-Hill Companies, ISBN 007141374X, $14.95).

Electronic Resumes and Online Networking: How to Use the Internet to Do a Better Job Search by Rebecca Smith (Career Press, Inc., ISBN 1564145115, $13.99).

e-Resumes: Everything You Need to Know About Using Electronic Resumes to Tap into Today's Hot Job Market by Susan Britton Whitcomb & Pat Kendall (The McGraw-Hill Companies, ISBN 0071363998, $11.95).

Recommended Web Sites

Yahoo! HotJobs Career Tools:
http://hotjobs.yahoo.com/careertools

Yahoo! HotJobs Salary Calculator:
http://hotjobs.yahoo.com/salary

Better Business Bureau:
www.bbb.org

George Mason University Portfolio:
An Effective Way to Showcase Your Skills and Experiences:
http://careers.gmu.edu/students/jobhunt/portfolio.cfm

Internet Fraud Complaint Center:
www.ifccfbi.gov

U.S. Department of Labor's Occupational Outlook Handbook:
www.bls.gov/oco

University of Oklahoma Job Evaluation Matrix:
http://ou.placementmanual.com/jobsearch/jobsearch-04.html

Weddles.com Tips for Success:
www.weddles.com/tips/seekers.htm

CHAPTER 6

Why Can't We Be Friends?:
Creating and Maintaining
a Network

"Hi. I'm, I'm, I'm . . . You'll have to forgive me, I'm terrible with names."

In the mid-1990s, actor Kevin Bacon's career had become so successful that it spawned a party game called "Six Degrees of Kevin Bacon." Players traced movie stars back to Kevin Bacon through his many flicks—and the connections they could make (such as Priscilla Presley and O.J. Simpson) were often pretty amazing.

The game was a takeoff on the phrase "six degrees of separation," referring to the theory that you have a connection to every other person on the planet through six or fewer people you know.

Take the Web site Friendster.com, for example, which connects you to "friends of friends of friends." The site has millions of members—and it all started with just a handful of people. This illustrates just how powerful a personal network can be. In addition, you never know who might be in it—if your cousin's girlfriend works for a rock star, that star is in your network! If your best friend's hairstylist's brother is your state's governor, then the governor is in your network.

The word *network* may sound boring to some and daunting to others, conjuring up images of stuffy people in suits shaking hands and trading business cards. But a network is merely a group of people you know, who know other people, who in turn are linked to other people—all of whom are potential contacts with job leads for you!

You may think that your network is composed only of your friends and coworkers from Funtastic Fried Chicken, and that they can't possibly help you find a job.

But they can. Because they too have friends, family, and neighbors—all of whom could lead to jobs. In addition, you can expand your network even more simply by chatting with the person standing next to you at the airport. Imagine! He could be the president of the local bank, a dot-com pioneer, or the human resources director of your favorite sports team. You just never know.

And this is key: **The Society of Human Resources Management estimates that 60–80 percent of jobs are filled through word-of-mouth.** A network is truly the most important weapon in your job-hunting arsenal. Yes, you should continue to search on the Internet and using other methods; just don't get so comfy behind that computer monitor that you don't get out and meet *people* who could lead you to a job.

In this chapter, we'll show you why a network is such a powerful and important tool. We'll also show you how to enlarge your network with people who can point you toward the fields and jobs you will love!

From the Desk of

Clent Richardson
Chief Marketing Officer, Nortel

Relationships are critical to your success and career management. Skills, education, training, and experience are important to show a track record, but they don't show potential or capability. I've found the people and the relationships one has are the ultimate differentiator in finding, securing, and being successful in jobs.

I've been fortunate to identify mentors and "career guides" whom I've used for advice and counsel, and to this day these are individuals whom I respect, trust, and go to—because I know that they will give me caring and candid advice. They have my best interest at heart, so they tell me not what I want to hear, but what they know I need to hear.

Very early on in my career when I was very young, I was asked by the chairman of a large, global telecommunications firm, "What do you want to do?" I told him, "I can do whatever you want me to do." The response I got was polite, but firm: "You need to know what you want to do, and then I can help you." The lesson there is to know the answer, have a plan, and show initiative. Know your business and how you can add value. Don't ask the big questions and not have the answers.

When I hire, I look for people who have a proven track record. Education is about discipline and a gauge for future success. To be clear, my focus is on potential and capability. I look for someone who really knows a critical area, as well as for confidence. I want someone who is efficient and articulate and can simplify big concepts. I'm looking for the big thinkers, the ones with the big ideas.

In a new grad, I would be looking for someone who is balanced in their approach to life—not only do they excel at academics, but they also have hobbies, outside interests, and are well-rounded. I look for high energy, hustle, and attitude. I also want folks who are grounded and have perspective—broad cultural experience is a perfect example. I want to see that they can adapt and change quickly. And I am drawn to drive and determination that is summarized as: They don't know they can't! The journey for the right job and the right career is one of the hardest and most rewarding jobs anyone can have. So, get in the driver's seat, manage your own career, and do what others could not even imagine.

take a memo

What Is SHRM?

The Society for Human Resource Management (SHRM) is the world's largest association devoted to human resource management. With nearly 200,000 members, SHRM has as its mission to provide comprehensive resources to the human resources community and to ensure that HR personnel are informed and effective in developing and educating companies' staffs.

SHRM (www.shrm.org) follows trends in hiring and management of staffs as well as recognizes companies with diverse and innovative approaches to hiring. It's a wonderful resource for you, as a new job seeker, if you want to know, for example, the latest news on company health care coverage, or what the best small- to medium-sized companies to work for are, or simply for insight from recruiters on how you can become better at interviewing and writing resumes. Much of the site's content is available for free online.

HOW NETWORKING WORKS

There is a reason sheep, buffalo, prairie dogs, and even lions live in groups: Working together is safer and more effective than working alone.

You need a group on your side to help link you to jobs, not to mention give you the support and encouragement you will need along the way. And the process is very easy to start.

Let's say you are currently an economics major hoping to find a job managing budgets. You let three people know about your hopes:

1. Professor Smith, your senior economics professor
2. Mr. Jenkins, your longtime next-door neighbor
3. Colleen, your best friend

Professor Smith calls her cousin, Janice, the vice president of a bank in Chicago—one of the cities where you hope to relocate. There are no jobs right now, but the bank plans to launch a new line of products in the fall and will be looking for entry-level help. It also happens that Janice's next-door neighbor is looking to rent out a one-bedroom basement apartment.

Mr. Jenkins gives your resume to the head of a nonprofit for which he volunteers. There is a job available in communications—not your specialty, but it does still involve working with the group's budgets.

Colleen's stepmom is assistant manager of a gift shop and needs some part-time help.

So there—just by talking to three people you already have leads on two full-time positions, a place to live, and a part-time job in the meantime to help you get by while you think things through.

Finding leads won't go this smoothly every time, but start the ball rolling. You never know what possibilities will come back to you in two weeks, two months, even two years. So let people know about your interests, stay in touch with them, and keep them posted on your progress.

▶**Action Items:** List at least one person in each of the following categories who could serve as a member of your personal network:

Family _____

Friends _____

Classmates _____

Professors _____

Neighbors _____

Former Supervisors _____

Volunteer Organizations _____

Houses of Worship _____

Coworkers _____

WHY YOU NEED TO NET A NETWORK

Employers Respect and Use Networks

Imagine that you are a hiring manager. Your department must meet certain sales targets the next quarter—who would you rather interview, a stranger. . . or someone referred to you by one of your most accomplished salespeople?

Employers trust networks because they take some of the unknown out of the hiring equation. As we mentioned in chapter 2, the hiring manager has a lot of pressure to find the right workers—mistakes can be costly. Anything (or, rather, anyone) that helps prove your worth makes the hiring manager feel more confident in you as a potential hire.

This is especially true when your advocate is already employed by a company where you'd like to work. A current employee knows not only you, but also the company culture and whether or not you'd make a good fit. Having this person endorse you can move your resume to the top of the hiring manager's pile.

Networks Give You the Inside Scoop
When a Job Becomes Available
If you hear about a job from a neighbor, you may get a chance to apply for it before it is even posted. Better yet, the neighbor can personally hand your resume to the recruiter or hiring manager. This saves you time and gives you an edge over other applicants. You can also find out more details about the position that you can use to tailor your resume and cover letter.

Networks Save You Time and Effort
Someone—a fellow alumnus, a neighbor, a family member—who can "get you in" can help you circumvent much of the red tape other applicants have to work their way through, such as submitting their resumes and trying to impress recruiters (who are meanwhile sizing up other candidates) before they reach the hiring manager. And of course, eliminating red tape saves you frustration and time—time you can use to seek other jobs.

Networks Give You Support and Guidance
Networks not only provide you with support and encouragement, but they give you a sounding board for ideas and suggestions. You can learn from your contacts' experiences. You can use them to help you practice your "elevator speech" and interview questions. And what is most important, they will give you support when you are feeling discouraged.

▶**Action Items:** On your computer or in a special job-hunting notebook, begin to develop a list of e-mail addresses called your "Network"—you can do so by expanding on the list of contacts you created earlier in the chapter. Group them according to "Friends," "Family," "Professors," and so forth. Send periodic e-mails **personalized** to each recipient, letting him or her know how your search is going.

Put together a timeline for how often to e-mail or call people in each group. Perhaps you check in with professors monthly, but family and friends weekly.

How Do I Build and Grow a Network?

First, you can take comfort in knowing that you already have a bigger network than you think!

Everyone you know or have ever known could potentially hold the key to a job for you. No, they might not be able to hire you themselves, but they might know or work for someone who can. Even though you haven't been in the working world yet (which will help boost your network exponentially), people in your life now—parents, friends, neighbors, professors, former supervisors, and so on—can help you find a job. These are also the people who know and love you best and will likely be the most willing to help you.

But it's not enough. You still need to expand your network even more. So where do you go?

take a memo

Recruiter Cheat Sheet: Working Your Network

Take note of these practical tips from Amy Costa, Specialty Recruiting Manager for professional services firm BearingPoint:

Work smarter not harder. To spread the word quickly, let everyone in your social network know that you are looking for a job.

First impressions are everything. Build a good rapport with contacts; ask them what they do and casually let them know that you are on the job market—even if they are not in the industry where you'd like to find a job.

Be in with the Internet. Use electronic networking tools to build your contacts.

Forge the alma mater connection. Reach out to alumni from your college or university, including social or academic clubs to which you belonged.

Build the rolodex. When you meet a new contact, ask for a business card to build your connections.

Happy "happy hours." Look in city papers, local magazines, and the Internet for calendar listings of networking events.

For the remainder of this chapter, we'll explore ways to build your personal network, as well as some useful tips for working your network to your advantage. We'll also look at some important considerations for maintaining your network even after you've found employment.

Alumni Groups and Events

First, be sure to join yours. And don't just stop at college—if your high school has a group, join it and keep your contact information updated.

There are two main ways to network with alumni:

1. Formal alumni networking events and directories
2. General alumni events

Formal networking events and directories are designed especially for new graduates to put you in touch with fellow graduates. Call your alumni office for help in locating nearby alums, or, if the alumni directory is online, you can search for graduates in your region to set up informational interviews. Keep your information current and if you have trouble finding someone nearby, contact your alumni office for help.

Alumni social gatherings, such as monthly dinners, seminars, or volunteer events, are more about fun and sharing networking opportunities. These help you meet people in a more informal environment and can be preferable for introverts who feel uncomfortable approaching people directly about jobs. Brian, a job seeker in Nashville, actually went to an alumni event for his *girlfriend* and met one of her fellow alumni, who brought him in for an interview the next week!

Even if your college doesn't have a local chapter, consider attending the next big event in a nearby city.

Forget What Your Parents Taught You— You *Do* Need to Talk to Strangers

You don't have to go door to door, but consider talking to the person next to you on the plane instead of listening to your iPod. When the Chamber of Commerce has a dinner, make a point of attending and talking to the keynote speaker.

Maybe you don't like the idea of chatting with "grown-ups," but—surprise! You're one yourself now. And, as we've said before, people like to talk about themselves and help college graduates—especially when they have college-age kids of their own. What is more important, all older workers have been faced with finding that first job. So they can empathize.

Outside the Box

A Lifetime of Contacts

If you're well beyond college, but are looking to start a new career with an entry-level job, networking is a fantastic option for you. Your age and experience can place you ahead of younger counterparts! You may be less easily intimidated and have a bigger network of friends and former coworkers. So ask around—who has contacts with the jobs that interest you? Can a friend help you set up an informational interview with her manager? People will be happy to help you—even if you're not a kid anymore.

Networking Groups/Job Clubs

These groups exist for the express purpose of helping their members find jobs. Some are general job-seeking groups, such as Pink Slip Parties (free events thrown all over the United States by the Hired Guns Marketing Consulting Group to bring together those who have lost their jobs with recruiters and career coaches), while others are geared toward a specific occupation, industry, or career stage.

If you're shy or unsure about how to get started, structured networking groups may be the answer. With the help of facilitators, employed peers, and career coaches, these organizations offer opportunities for members to connect and share job leads. Structured networking groups teach networking techniques in a safe, nonthreatening forum. They are usually categorized by profession, income, or geography.

You'll have to do some research to find the group that's right for you. You can find out when and where networking groups and job clubs are meeting in local newspaper listings or on the groups' Web sites.

Industry Organizations

Industry organizations (or "trade organizations") exist for just about every field you could imagine (even animal trainers and cowboys have them). Although they require annual dues, many do take recent college grads' status—and pocket-book—into account. The Society for Professional Journalists, for example, invites "College Student/Post Grad" candidates to join for under $40 per year.

Depending on where you live, there are also free, local groups that develop around certain industries—such as women in technology, filmmakers, and writers. Search the Web for local chapters and events you can attend free or nearly free of charge.

Web Communities

Similar to the "live" groups, you can also find many online communities for trading job information and advice. Use Web chat rooms and job boards like Yahoo! Groups (http://groups.yahoo.com) and Yahoo! HotJobs Communities (www.hotjobs.com/htdocs/client/splash/communities) to "talk" with other job seekers.

Volunteer Groups

Volunteering can be a great way to network. Not only are you meeting like-minded people, but you're also learning new skills that you can apply to the real world.

For example, Eric had been working at a bookstore when he began volunteering for a local politician's campaign. The politician lost her race, but the chief-of-staff for a congressman in the district needed help with speechwriting, and had heard about Eric's hard work—and hired him!

 **THINK Outside the Box**

Alternative Ways to Get Business Cards

Business cards are still a tried and true way of recording contacts' information—and allowing them to record yours. But without a job, you don't have business cards.

Not a problem—simply print up some simple ones on nice card stock from your own computer, or have some inexpensive ones printed at a local print shop or one of the Web sites listed below. They don't need to be fancy—they just need to have your name, phone number, and e-mail address. New contacts will respect your spunkiness, and the cards give you something tangible to hand to new contacts and spare you the embarrassment of digging for a pen and a scrap of paper. Here are some useful sites you don't want to miss:

- www.vistaprint.com
- www.iprint.com

take a memo

Networking Dos and Don'ts

Before you head out to the alumni or network group meet-and-greet, keep these tips in mind:

The Four Most Common Networking Mistakes:

- ☼ This is not a party. Yes, there may be food and even alcohol, but you are here first and foremost to find a job.
- ☼ Don't neglect your homework. Find out who is throwing the event. Then research them and any keynote speakers—and *meet them!*
- ☼ Don't forget to give your elevator speech.
- ☼ Focus on the quality, not quantity, of your connections—you'll get better results from that than handing out business cards indiscriminately.

Four Networking Dos:

- ☼ **Family First:** Practice your pitch on your family.
- ☼ **Friends in Need:** Don't just talk about job searching at job events— *any* gathering of friends is an opportunity to let people know that you're job hunting.
- ☼ **Presenting . . . You!:** Make sure your presentation is impeccable— dress appropriately for the event, use breath mints, have a firm handshake, and take plenty of business cards and resumes.
- ☼ **Networking Goes Digital:** Use the Web to network—such as through job sites, interest groups, and job boards. If you see a job you don't want, pass it on to someone who does.

TIPS TO TAKE WITH YOU

Here are some useful pointers to get you started.

Play up the College Grad Angle

If you're a current college student or recent grad, you are in a fortunate position to network compared to other job seekers. People who are employed can't talk as freely about looking for a job. But new grads are expected to be job hunting, so they can spread the news of their search far and wide.

Don't Be Afraid to Ask for Help

Don't assume that your contacts know you're job hunting. Tell people that you're looking for a job and ask if they know anyone who can help. Do they know anyone in the fields you are interested in? Would they mind taking a business card? Also contact your former professors and supervisors from previous part-time work or volunteer work for ideas and more contacts. Send periodic personalized e-mails to members of your network about how your search is going. (See the exercise on page 78.)

A Word to Introverts

Maybe you're thinking, sure, networking's easy if you are outgoing! But I'm not good at meeting new people!

As we've pointed out, you don't have to meet new people to start a successful network. Your friends and neighbors alone can be a good start.

But ultimately that won't be enough. You have to go beyond the people you know and begin "selling yourself" to strangers who can hold the key to your future.

Don't worry; it's not as painful as it sounds. Use e-mail to network with new people without having to go face to face. Ask your friends to help introduce you to people who can help you, and then to stay there with you to facilitate conversation—and to brag about your strengths.

Also, challenge yourself in small increments. Go to a party, a networking event, or a community event, and talk to one person for five minutes—make sure to mention that you are looking for a job! That's all, just five little minutes, and then you can excuse yourself. Maybe in those five minutes you'll get a lead on a job, maybe not. At the very least you'll have met someone new who now has you in mind should a matching job ever come his way.

▶**Action Items:** Every week, set yourself a goal of making one new contact. Go to a community event—a Chamber of Commerce meet-and-greet, even a concert—and get to know one person. Or, go on an informational interview. Call your mom's sorority sister who now owns a bookstore. Find just one person you can add to your network, and find out who they know—especially those in the field in which you are interested. Then begin contacting those people—challenge yourself to find the right one!

MAINTAINING YOUR NETWORK

Just as with cars, networks require some "regular maintenance." However, the time required is minimal compared to the payoff. It only takes a few moments to send out an e-mail congratulating a friend on his engagement or to make a phone call inquiring about a contact's new baby. In a later conversation, you can remind them you are still looking.

Keep notes on your contacts' interests, birthdays, life events—these will give you a legitimate reason to contact them from time to time, and give you something to discuss beyond "What can you do for me?" People are immediately turned off by someone who appears to be in it only for himself.

Don't Forget to Return the Favor

If you see a job that would interest people in your network, or even just another good contact for them, pass it on. Arrange a dinner for people in your network to meet one another.

It seems that the more you try and help others, the more it comes back to you. Be on the lookout as you develop your network for ways you can help people within it. You would be surprised at the connections you can foster. For example, you might not be able to find your dad's best friend a job, but maybe you can arrange a college interview for his son who's a senior in high school.

And When I Find a Job?

The second-worst mistake you can make, next to not having a network at all, is to let yours lapse once you do find a job. Don't rest on your laurels once that offer letter is signed. Things change quickly these days. Stocks are up and down, executives come and go—and companies fluctuate as a result. Perfectly wonderful employees are sometimes let go simply to keep the business afloat.

So stay in touch with your contacts—let them know how happy you are in your new position, and ask whether there is anything you can do for them. Then when you do change jobs—either by choice or necessity, you'll already have a network in place to help you find the next position.

Recommended Books

The Networking Survival Guide: Get the Success You Want by Tapping Into the People You Know by Diane Darling (The McGraw-Hill Companies, ISBN 0071409998, $14.95).

Never Eat Alone: And Other Secrets to Success, One Relationship at a Time by Keith Ferrazzi (Doubleday & Company, Inc., ISBN 0385512058, $24.95).

Dig Your Well Before You're Thirsty: The Only Networking Book You'll Ever Need by Harvey Mackay (Doubleday & Company, Inc., ISBN 0385485468, $15.95).

The Referral of a Lifetime (The Ken Blanchard Series): The Networking System that Produces Bottom-line Results . . . Every Day! by Tim Templeton (Berrett-Koehler Publishers, Inc., ISBN 1576752402, $19.95).

A Foot in the Door: Networking Your Way into the Hidden Job Market by Katherine Hansen (Ten Speed Press, ISBN 1580081401, $14.95).

How to Make People Like You in 90 Seconds or Less by Nicholas Boothman (Workman Publishing Company, Inc., ISBN 076111940X, $14.95).

How to Win Friends and Influence People by Dale Carnegie (Simon & Schuster, ISBN 0671723650, $7.99).

Recommended Web Sites

Yahoo! Groups:
http://groups.yahoo.com

Yahoo! Message Boards:
http://messages.yahoo.com

Yahoo! People Search:
http://people.yahoo.com

eHow—How to Make Small Talk:
www.ehow.com/how_10812_make-small-talk.html

The Pink Slip Party:
www.thehiredguns.com/events

Salary.com—Networking to Find a Job:
www.salary.com

The Shyness Home page:
www.shyness.com

Weddles.com Association Directory:
www.weddles.com/associations

CHAPTER 7

Now Introducing . . . You!:
All About Cover Letters

*"You come highly recommended, young man,
but what experience have you had besides helping
your mother around the house?"*

Just how important are cover letters? Forty-three percent of recruiters surveyed by the Society for Human Resource Management say cover letters are just as important as resumes.

Why are these few paragraphs so significant?

A cover letter helps the recruiter—and therefore helps you. The recruiter receives dozens of resumes, and may be looking to fill several jobs at the same time. A solid cover letter will not only set you apart, but make you more memorable to a recruiter when she needs to hone those dozens of resumes down to four or five.

A cover letter gives you room for style and personality. Your resume is, by necessity, a pretty straightforward document with little room for flavor. A cover letter, however, gives you a chance to speak to a recruiter, as a normal person, and show him that you are more than just words on a page, but an informed, serious job seeker hoping to help his company. (Plus you get to write *real sentences* instead of bullet points.)

A cover letter can highlight information not included in your resume. There are some accomplishments you have had that might be too detailed to fully explain on a resume. A cover letter is a chance to fill in the blanks. In addition, a cover letter allows you to relate your experience to the specific company and your interest in working there, any special circumstances, your relocation preferences, and other such details.

A cover letter lets you "show your stuff." Much like your elevator speech noted in chapter 3, the cover letter *succinctly* highlights your top skills and accomplishments—and invites the reader to learn more by reading your resume. This is your cover letter's ultimate goal, after all—getting the recruiter to read the resume!

In all, a solid cover letter sends a single, important message to a potential employer—that you are a qualified candidate for the job. A recruiter can get a good idea of how well you fit the job just by glancing at your great cover letter before even reading your resume. What recruiter wouldn't appreciate that?

PREPARING TO WRITE THE COVER LETTER

Your cover letter is less about *you* than about how you match up with the job being advertised. So before you start writing, first make some notes—you want to customize your letter as much as possible, not just bang out a form letter. Recruiters will spot that a mile away.

take a memo

Electronic versus Paper Cover Letters

In today's electronic age, you will likely be sending out more e-mail cover letters than paper ones. Because we use e-mail so much, and because recruiters prefer it (a whopping 83 percent of recruiters surveyed by HotJobs prefer receiving resumes via e-mail), it's easy to think that a quick sentence or nothing at all is acceptable to accompany your resume.

But you should be just as careful when writing an e-mail cover letter as you would writing a paper cover letter. Here are some tips:

- ☼ Be polite and professional—don't use slang, emoticons, or add graphics or philosophical quotes at the bottom.
- ☼ Use spell-check.
- ☼ Follow traditional business letter conventions, even though you're sending your letter electronically.
- ☼ Include your full contact information.
- ☼ Attach your resume and work samples, if requested. If you are linking to work samples, double-check the hyperlinks.

Take a copy of the job description you're applying for and carefully read it over several times. Note parallels between your own skills and those required for the position.

Many job descriptions also mention software with which applicants should be familiar. Be sure to take an inventory of your own software skills and note which of these match up with the job description. The same goes for other hard and soft skills, as well as your "work quirks."

Make an outline of how your skills and experience match up with the job. This will also help when it's time to tailor your resume to the job. Ask yourself: *What does the job description prioritize as the primary responsibilities?* Pick out the strongest parallels and list them in the order you'd like to address them.

You may find that you have a lot to include in your cover letter. That, by the way, is a good sign that you're a strong candidate for the job. But it's important to feature only the strongest points in your cover letter, since the letter should be no longer than one page.

WRITING THE LETTER

The body of a cover letter can be broken down into three basic parts:

- ☼ **Opening (1–2 paragraphs):** Here is where you introduce yourself, state the job you are applying for—be sure you include the job title as it is listed in the job advertisement along with any identifying codes—and why you are interested in it.

- ☼ **What You Can Do for the Company (1–2 paragraphs):** Here you further explain what you have to offer, *not what the company can do for you.* Using the job advertisement as your guide, highlight your skills and accomplishments that match those being sought by the employer. Do not rehash your entire resume.

- ☼ **Why You Should Work Together (1 paragraph):** Summarize why you would make a great addition to their team and how you have more information to back that up. Include a time you will call to follow up.

You'll also need a header (recruiter's name and title, company, address, and salutation) and a conclusion ("Sincerely, Mike Miller").

The conclusion is pretty simple, but for salutations, be sure to address a person, not "To Whom It May Concern." Get a name either from the job ad, the company Web site, or even by calling the company and asking for a recruiter in the human resources department. If you absolutely cannot find a name, then address the letter to "Dear Recruiter" or "Dear Human Resources Director." Never say "Dear Sir" or "Dear Madam"—you don't know which gender will ultimately wind up reading your letter.

Section One: The Grand Opening

Journalists are taught to begin every story they write with a strong lead paragraph—a punchy, sharp opening that immediately draws in readers and keeps them reading.

take a memo

From the Mouth of a Hiring Manager

"The quickest way to sort the pile [of resumes] is by glancing at cover letters to see if they refer to specific skill sets from the ad. I'm dismayed by how many applicants spotlight their favorite talent in their cover letter ('I'm great with people,' 'I love writing') even though it's not a skill our ad mentioned.

"So there they are singing and dancing about how wonderful they are at something, but it's not the thing my ad very specifically said we were looking for. The tiny percent who took the time to craft a letter that said, 'I'm great at X, Y, Z that you say you want' are the ones who we call for interviews."

—Anne Holland, Publisher, MarketingSherpa

The same applies to your cover letter. For your first sentence you want a strong opening—not "My name is..." (that's already noted in several places) or "Hello, I'm applying for XYZ job."

Yes, you absolutely need to state the job for which you are applying, and the sooner the better—a recruiter shouldn't have to read your entire letter just to know what job you're applying for. Just do so in a catchy way:

Dear Mr. Jeffords,
An efficient office has an efficient leader running it. I would like to be that leader as the next Office Manager for Acme, per your job ad # X47KD, as listed on Yahoo! HotJobs.

The leadoff sentence needs to grab the recruiter's attention and make a statement about you. Here are some approaches you can use:

Referral: Remember that great network you've been building? Now's the chance to use it:

Dear Ms. Landry,
Your regional vice president, Tom Allenby, suggested that I contact you. He feels that my pre-veterinary degree and interest in researching canine dental care could be of good use to your pet products line.

(This mentions a company contact and relates company business to your experience and interests.)

take a memo

Who's Who?

Honorifics like *Mr.* and *Mrs.* are preferred by some, but not by others. Be sensitive to this, as well as people who might have professional honorifics such as "Dr."

If you are addressing a woman, simply use *Ms.*

If you cannot decipher whether the recruiter's name belongs to a man or a woman (as in "Kris," "Pat," or "Joe/Jo"), you can call the company and ask how to address your letter. If that doesn't work, you can use the person's full name, as in the greeting—"Dear Jo Martin."

Success Record: Here is where you can start off with strong proof of your past success in college or other ventures. Mention concrete numbers if possible:

> Dear Ms. Eagleton,
> As president of the Springfield University chapter of Habitat for Humanity, I oversaw the building of three new homes in the Springfield community.

(This mentions hard numbers, a leadership position, and a brand name.)

General Knowledge: Demonstrate a broad understanding of the field in which you're applying:

> Dear Mr. Johnson,
> With the growth of home and garden television shows, the home candle retail industry has seen sales growth of more than 20 percent during the last five years.

(This shows you are on top of the trends.)

News-related: Mention an article or television piece about the company (not one about a scandal, however):

> Dear Ms. Boynton,
> The July 24 *New York Times* article about Acme's new line of rust-proof anvils intrigued me, as I researched iron compounds while earning my chemistry degree.

(This gives the date and place of the article, and relates the company's business to your experience.)

THINK Outside the Box

The Humorous Opening—A Comedy of Errors

Use a humorous or informal opening with *extreme* caution—only if you truly know and understand the company for which you are applying. For example, certain companies, like those in advertising or graphic design, might appreciate creativity or humor in a cover letter—as long as it also demonstrates a solid knowledge of their industry:

> Who is able to leap tall buildings in a single bound? Well, not me, but with my Adobe Illustrator expertise, I would make a "super" addition to the graphic design staff at Superguy Comics, Inc.

(Starts off funny but gets right to the point.)

Section Two: Why You Are Great for the Job

Here's the fun part—now you finally get to talk about some of those hard and soft skills you've been cataloging, and how they work in the context of the job you're applying for.

A few things to remember:

Keep your sentences clear and brief. According to SHRM, recruiters spend an average of sixty seconds or less reading cover letters—don't give them a reason to spend any less time on yours.

Refer to, but don't rehash, your resume. Rather, select your two or three best accomplishments and relate them to the job for which you are applying. You can always discuss other accomplishments (which are listed in your resume, anyway) in an interview.

Also, if you're applying for a job you found in an ad, **be sure to refer to the ad's requirements here**. If the ad asks for MS Office, and you know those programs, say so. If the ad asks for Quark, or proven experience in leading a team, specify your experience there, too. Mention the skills by name—even quote the job ad word for word.

Now let's see what the body of your letter looks like when you keep the above points in mind. Perhaps you're applying for an entry-level position with an interior design firm. The firm seeks a "self-starter" with "first-rate communication skills." You might say:

I recently received my degree in art history from Richardson University, and successfully completed an internship with Parker and Miller Interiors in Ann Arbor, Michigan. As a hard-working self-starter with first-rate communication skills . . .

Or for an executive assistant position with desktop publishing and WinXP experience:

As secretary for the Panhellenic Council at Adams State University, I oversaw meeting planning and fund-raising, as well as published the group's monthly newsletter using Windows XP.

Section Three: Working Together

Your final paragraph should fuse your skills and the company's needs—showing how you could work well together to enhance the company's success. For example:

I believe my experience in designing Web pages for the nonprofit industry would benefit the clients you represent, such as G.I.V.E. and the Food Pantry. Not only can my familiarity with user interface and graphic design help your firm continue to meet the needs of your current client base, but I can also help bring in new business.

Make certain to offer to contact the recruiter within the next week to follow up. Give your contact information should he or she want to contact you in the meantime:

I would appreciate an opportunity to meet with you to discuss this position. I will call you next Monday, July 25, to follow up. In the meantime, you can reach me at 555-5555.

> *Sincerely,*
> *Sandy Alvarez*

A brief note about following up: Sometimes a job ad won't give a phone number or will specifically state "no phone calls." Recruiters do this to manage their time and avoid being inundated by calls from job seekers.

It's best to approach with caution. Consider following up first via e-mail. Explain you simply want to be certain they received your resume. (Even if the ad does not give an e-mail address, you can likely find the HR department e-mail address by visiting the company Web site.) If that fails to garner a response, feel free to call the company switchboard (also on the Web site) and ask for the human resources department. Again, state who you are and the job for which you have applied, and ask if there is anything else they need from you. Be brief and polite—no one can fault you for wanting to know your next steps.

take a memo

Don't Become a Cover Letter Statistic

A badly written cover letter can hurt your chances. More than 76 percent of recruiters said in a recent SHRM survey that they would not consider a cover letter with typos, or at best they would toss the accompanying resume into a file rather than consider it for that current job. And 61 percent said the same about cover letters addressed to the wrong company.

The most common cover letter blunders are usually related to one of the following:

Name That Job: Recruiters may be filling more than one job simultaneously. After greeting him or her, state exactly which job you're applying for.

Form Letters: The point of a cover letter is to make a personal connection with the reader. Tailor your letter specifically to each company you send it to.

Don't Repeat Yourself: Don't regurgitate everything that's in your resume—offer deeper insights into what your resume does not say. Provide an in-depth explanation of some of your key achievements at your last job, for instance, and how those accomplishments could help the company. Or tell a story about a tough problem you solved.

What Can You Do for Me?: Don't say you are applying for the job for money, travel, or anything else that concerns only you.

Balance Confidence and Humility: While you certainly want to appear competent, arrogance can turn a recruiter off: "Throw away all those other resumes—I'm your guy!" Show enthusiasm and a positive attitude, but don't overdo it.

THE FINAL PRODUCT

Now that you understand the components of a cover letter, let's put it all together.

Let's say you are a recent graduate, an English major who worked two summers at a gift shop, worked as an editor for the school newspaper, and also volunteered at a local after-school literacy program. You are applying for a position as a junior copywriter for a small ad firm. The job ad seeks someone who is deadline-oriented, creative, has fresh ideas and strong writing skills. The applicant must also be able to produce copy on tight deadlines and have a strong working knowledge of AP Style.

As you draw parallels between your experience and the job requirements, you realize:

- ☼ Being an English major requires writing skills and creativity.
- ☼ Volunteering at a literacy program requires communication, compassion, and also creativity.
- ☼ Working at the part-time job requires a good grasp of customer service, being able to meet deadlines, and knowing how to work on a team.

Guess what! You already have the basis for the skills this job seeks, and more!

Style Points to Remember

We've already mentioned some style points to keep in mind, but they are important enough to bear repeating:

- ☼ Don't open with "To Whom It May Concern"—get a name if possible
- ☼ Keep the letter to one page
- ☼ Highlight first and foremost the skills and experiences you have that match those the employer is seeking
- ☼ Open with a strong lead sentence
- ☼ Refer to the job ad and its specific language
- ☼ Offer to follow up with the recruiter
- ☼ For electronic letters, attach your resume and make sure any links you include work
- ☼ Proofread your work

Now for a few more:

- ☼ Use "power" words like "implemented," "performed," "strategized," and "facilitated." Also use active voice. That is, rather than "The rugby club's profits were raised 10 percent by me," say: "I raised the rugby team's fundraising profits by 10 percent."
- ☼ Make sure your language is not stiff, but not informal either.
- ☼ Don't call the recruiter by first name, even if you have met before.

Susie Brown
123 Main Street
Anytown, USA 12345

Jane Pelletier, Human Resources Director
Great Ads, Inc.
100 Main Street
Anytown, USA 55555

July 30, 2005

Dear Ms. Pelletier,

It was with great pleasure that I read in the July 22 *Anytown Times* that Great Ads, Inc., is expanding its business into the local restaurant industry. **[Opens with strong knowledge of the company]** I believe my experience in writing and restaurant service are a unique match for the Junior Copywriter position, #XC77Y on HotJobs.com. **[States job title, number, and exactly why she is qualified to apply]**

As an English major at State University and editor for the school newspaper, I developed my creativity and writing skills in deadline-oriented environments and achieved strong working knowledge of AP Style. **[Mentions skills from the ad verbatim]** Volunteering with the Heads-Up literacy program helped me learn to make words exciting. **[Not mentioned in the ad but important to copywriting]**

Perhaps most important, as a server at several Anytown restaurants, I gained a valuable familiarity with the environments, patrons, and menus of the very businesses you seek to assist. **[Takes something as common as waiting tables and turns it into valuable business experience.]** I would appreciate the opportunity not only to write fresh ads for these restaurants, but perhaps to generate new business using my network of contacts at these locations. **[The possibility of new business? A hiring manager's dream!]**

I would appreciate an opportunity to meet with you to discuss the Junior Copywriter position. I will call you next Monday, August 8, to follow up. In the meantime, you can reach me at 555-5555. **[States follow-up information and date]**

Sincerely,
Susie Brown

Enclosure

☼ When touting your achievements, be confident but don't exaggerate, brag, or lie.

☼ If you're sending a paper cover letter, three lines below the closing, type "Enclosure" (referring to your resume). You'll look professional, detail-oriented, and oh-so-savvy.

☼ If you're sending a cover letter in the body of an e-mail, you may opt to begin with the salutation—rather than opening with your address and that of the recruiter, as with a traditional business letter.

BEFORE YOU HIT SEND

Some parting thoughts before you send that letter off into cyberspace: Proofread and spell-check your letter. Now do it again. Ask a friend or family member to read your cover letter for typos and grammatical errors. If you're stuck on a grammatical point, consult a grammar guide such as the classic *Elements of Style* by William Strunk, Jr. and E. B. White.

Finally, send the letter to yourself as a test to check formatting. If you find errors, correct them and read it one more time—it's so easy to overlook a mistake, and you don't want a typo ruining all your hard work.

A cover letter may be a brief document, but it's an important one. It introduces you to the recruiter and interests him in reading another important document—your resume. In chapter 8, we'll look at how to present your experience and skills in a winning resume.

Recommended Books

Writing a Resume and Cover Letter (Barnes & Noble Basics Series) by Susan Stellin (Silver Lining Books, ISBN 0760737924, $9.95).

Get the Interview Every Time: Fortune 500 Hiring Professionals' Tips for Writing Winning Resumes and Cover Letters by Brenda Greene (Dearborn, ISBN 0793183022, $12.95).

Cover Letters for Dummies by Joyce Lain Kennedy (John Wiley & Sons, Inc., ISBN 0764552244, $16.99).

Gallery of Best Cover Letters: A Collection of Quality Cover Letters by Professional Resume Writers by David F. Noble (JIST Publishing, Inc., ISBN 1563709902, $18.95).

The Elements of Style by William Strunk, Jr. and E .B. White (Pearson Education, ISBN 020530902X, $7.95).

Recommended Web Sites

George Mason University's Job Search Letters:
http://careers.gmu.edu/students/jobhunt/letters.html

University of California at Berkeley's Boring Cover Letters:
http://career.berkeley.edu/Article/030912a.stm

Yahoo! HotJobs—Cover Letters:
http:/hotjobs.yahoo.com/resume

CHAPTER 8

Your Life Story in One Page: Resumes

"Thank you, sir. I __am__ proud of my resume.
And I think you'll find that most of it is true."

Writing a resume can give you a great sense of accomplishment. It is tangible proof of all the academic and professional accomplishments in your life so far.

Writing can also be a fearsome task. A resume is quite possibly the most important document you will write in your life.

As a new job seeker, you have the added burden of the pressure and uncertainty that comes with little to no experience in writing a resume. Not only are you unsure of format and style—even longtime employees feel that way—but *what the heck do you put on it?*

Guess what—you've likely already written most of what you need for your resume! If you've been doing the exercises thus far in this book, you have already documented many of your most notable work experiences, your soft and hard skills, and your "elevator speech."

In this chapter we'll show you how to craft a winning resume, one that represents the best of your personal and professional skills and will not only be read, but will also get you interviews.

Basic Resume Format

Your resume should reflect who you are—within reason. There's a great scene in the movie *Legally Blonde*, in which Reese Witherspoon's character submits a resume printed on pink, scented paper. Despite the raised eyebrows of her critics, her character goes on to succeed.

In real life, the resume is not a place to take chances. Your cover letter and interview give you more room to show your personality, but resumes don't offer much leeway. They have a standard format that recruiters like and expect, and therefore it's one you as a job seeker should follow.

However, take comfort in these limitations. By knowing that you can and should stick to tried and true methods, you can put your creative energies into describing your experience and skills instead of worrying about new ways to present them.

THE FORMATS

There are three common resume formats: chronological, functional, and *curriculum vitae.*

Chronological Format

Chronological format (sometimes called "reverse chronological" format) is by far the most popular way to construct a resume. It lists your work experience from most to least recent and provides dates and descriptions of each job. Recruiters prefer this format—84 percent said so in a Yahoo! HotJobs survey. It is easy to follow and shows your career progression through the years. (For an example of a resume that follows this format, see page 116, later in this chapter.)

Functional Format

Functional resumes are more ability-focused and do not follow chronological format. They are geared toward what the specific job requires and what the job seeker can do for the company rather than detailing a linear work history. While this may sound like a good idea, only certain job seekers should use the functional format—for example, a person who has some gaps in his or her career may want to overshadow that by grouping a resume by experience instead. While functional resumes are good for this purpose, recruiters may assume that by using the functional format you are trying to hide something.

Curriculum Vitae (CV)

The CV is an extensive listing of experience and can be as long as ten pages or more. It is used in Europe and professional occupations such as medicine and academia—professions that involve many facets of work, such as ongoing education and research, writing, teaching, public speaking, areas of practice, and the like. You do not need to worry about a CV if you are seeking an entry-level job.

In addition to these formats there are also hybrids that you may use in future job searches. However, for our purposes we will focus on the chronological format because it is the format with which recruiters are most familiar and the one they prefer. In the pages that follow, we'll discuss what to include on your resume, how to organize the information, and how to handle some of the challenges that often plague first-time job seekers.

▶ ▲ ◀
hot facts •
▶ ▼ ◀

When Time Is Not on Your Side

The majority of recruiters spend less than three minutes reviewing a resume, according to a survey conducted by the Society for Human Resource Management. The easier you make it for them, the better chance you'll have of them reading your resume!

What to Put on It—and How

Now it's time to put your experience into a clear, concise, and powerful format. But before we begin, a few words about the resume's appearance.

Don't Be Fancy

You don't need graphics, odd fonts, or special software to write a resume. It's the content and the clarity that matter more than the aesthetics.

You can pay a designer to do a professional layout of your resume, but basic word processing software such as Microsoft Word is perfectly acceptable. Use a common font such as Arial or Times New Roman, and avoid hard-to-read or informal fonts such as **Comic Sans**. Use high-quality white or cream paper. With the exception of those in creative/artistic professions, don't include graphics or other "bells and whistles."

Do Keep Your Resume to One Page If Possible

In a recent Yahoo! HotJobs survey, more than 53 percent of recruiters said it was acceptable for a resume to be longer than one page, 41 percent said it was acceptable only if the applicant had extensive experience, and 6 percent said it was not acceptable. In other words, recruiters seem to feel that the length of the resume should reflect the experience of the candidate. As your experience grows, so can the length of your resume.

Do Make It Easy to Read

Recruiters may look at hundreds of resumes for every job they fill—a huge block of text is unappealing. Keep your words concise, use boldface, italics, bullet points, and white space to set off one section from another (and spread your experience out a little if it's somewhat thin).

Basic Arrangement of a Chronological Resume

A chronological resume follows a basic pattern:

- ☼ Contact information
- ☼ Objective Statement or Qualifications Summary
- ☼ Experience from most to least recent
- ☼ Skills
- ☼ Education
- ☼ Awards and Honors, Volunteer Work, Activities

take a memo

The Magic Bullet

A well-organized resume allows recruiters to quickly find what they're looking for. Bullet points help organize information into nuggets and make resumes more manageable.

Use them sparingly—try to summarize an experience in five bullet points or fewer. Also, avoid repetition as in the following:

- ☼ Writing GUI-based documentation
- ☼ Writing conceptual, procedural, and reference documents
- ☼ Writing Quick Reference Guides

The resume writer sampled above could have condensed these into one bullet:

- ☼ Write GUI-based documentation; Quick Reference Guides; and conceptual, procedural, and reference documents.

Or, he could have used words other than *writing*.

- ☼ Write GUI-based documentation
- ☼ Develop conceptual, procedural, and reference documents
- ☼ Create and implement Quick Reference Guides

Many new graduates list their education ahead of experience on their resume. This is perfectly fine, especially if you sense that the employer values an applicant's educational background (and if you feel you lack relevant experience). Also, if you attended a top-tier school or received an award such as a Rhodes Scholarship, you will want to list that higher on the resume. Bottom line, whatever you feel is most important to the employer—list that first.

Let's briefly review each section and what it requires.

CONTACT INFORMATION

This is, of course, your name, home address, phone number, and e-mail address. Be sure to use an e-mail address without a cutesy name—"FoxyGal" or "HugeGiantsFan" just won't do. If you're currently a student, as you list contact information, consider where you will be physically located—your parents' home or elsewhere? Will your phone number and e-mail address change after you graduate? You want employers to be able to reach you quickly and easily.

Objective and Summary Statements

The objective statement consists of one to two sentences at the beginning of your resume stating what you have to offer a company. It's a version of your elevator speech (see page 37), but condensed into a brief statement.

There is a debate over whether or not to list an objective statement. On the "pro" side, it helps the job seeker target a specific position, and demonstrates that you know what you want professionally. On the "con" side, an objective can limit you to just one position when you might be qualified for others.

Standard Objective Statement

The standard **objective statement** works well for those who are certain of what job they want to pursue, and those whose career goal is not clear in their resume.

Place the objective directly under your name and contact information. It should be simple, specific, and brief and should highlight what you have to offer the company, such as a specific skill or experience.

Remember to keep the focus on the company. New job seekers commonly think so narrowly about their search and what they need—such as rent money—that they forget that the company has needs too. Proper examples include:

- A position in which I can draw on my Web development skills to build exciting, informative Web sites in the health care industry.

Or,

- To use my marketing degree to help nonprofits boost donations and public exposure.

Do *not* use the following:

- To make money doing...
- To find a stepping-stone to...
- A position that allows casual hours and dress...

Review your objective each time you send out a resume and make sure it fits the job you're applying for. Just as you should have several versions of your resume, you should also have several versions of your job objective.

Summary Statement

If you're not sure of your career goals, another approach is the **summary statement**. While an objective focuses on the job, a summary statement focuses on the job seeker.

A summary statement is a one- to two-sentence overview that captures the essence of your skills and experience. It highlights what makes you a qualified candidate as well as what makes you different (and better) than other applicants.

Tailor your summary statement to highlight the experience that is most relevant to the job. Here's an example of a strong summary statement:

> **Summary:** *Communications major with experience managing campus-wide public relations campaigns, writing fraternity newsletter, and reporting on sports for the school newspaper.*

SUMMARY OF QUALIFICATIONS

Sometimes a job objective is too targeted, and a summary statement is too short to highlight all your accomplishments. However, you have another choice: the **summary of qualifications**. A summary of qualifications is a list of your most significant career accomplishments. It's most useful for job seekers who have a long work history or who are applying for senior positions. While generally less useful for a new grad, it's still an option worth exploring.

A summary of qualifications differs from a summary statement in two key ways:

1. It's formatted as a list of items rather than a single statement, and

2. It highlights specific accomplishments rather than general achievements.

This section also goes by many names, including "Key Accomplishments" and "Career Highlights."

For maximum effectiveness, the list should include no more than five items and be results-oriented. The summary of qualifications is usually a list of short phrases. You can use a bulleted list, with each qualification on its own line. Or, to conserve space, you can arrange them in paragraph format, with a period after each one. Here's an example of a bulleted list:

Summary of Qualifications
- Managed university bookstore with 20% revenue increase in 2005
- Skilled salesperson with three summers' experience at Sheila's Gifts and Goodies, Naperville, Ill.
- Internship with sales department, Acme Ads, Inc., Orlando, Fla.

Job objectives, summary statements, summaries of qualifications—all are useful resume options. Your best choice will depend on your experience and the type of job you're interested in.

EXPERIENCE

The experience section is the heart of the resume. Here is a plan to help you get the most out of it:

First, think about the accomplishments you've had thus far, either in your college career or in your work experiences. Consider

- Internships
- Classwork
- Sports
- Activities
- Part-time or full-time work, or work-study
- Volunteering

Next, on a notepad, list your experience in two columns: "Experience Relevant to this Specific Job" (skills mentioned in the job ad) and "Experience Relevant to This or Any Job" (skills such as speechwriting that might not be needed for a Web development job, but still demonstrate an aspect of your experience that could be valuable to the company in the future).

Remember that even if you planned sorority parties or played junior varsity tennis, these still involve skills that can be applied to the "real world" and should be counted as "experience" (budgeting, negotiation, leadership, and so forth).

Now under each experience/job, list its responsibilities and skills, as well as notable accomplishments/successes you achieved, for example "surpassed sales quota by 22 percent," or "trained three new employees in software system." Quantitative results—achievements that can be proven with hard numbers—demonstrate that you have a direct, positive effect on a company's bottom line.

Put a star by the ones that are relevant to the job you are applying for. Then pull out the starred items and list those in order of importance as they relate to the types of jobs you are seeking. For example, if you want to be a marketing assistant, then your Excel and PowerPoint skills and experience as fraternity treasurer would be items you'd want to list first.

Now transfer this information to the resume. Under "EXPERIENCE," list your work history in chronological order. For each job/experience, create bullet points for the starred items. They do not need to be full sentences. This will ultimately save you space. List the year or semester for each experience; for holiday work, specify the season: "Summer 2005."

You can have more than one bullet point for each experience, but make each bulleted item concise and powerful.

Let's consider the "Experience" section for a college graduate looking to land a job as a Web designer for a nonprofit:

EXPERIENCE
Developed award-winning Web sites for university, community, and commercial organizations.

Intern, Happy Cola Marketing Department, Atlanta, Georgia   Spring 2005
- Learned advanced Web development with award-winning Web design team for nation's No. 2 soft drink producer
- Coded HTML for "Intern Info," an intranet site for Happy Cola interns
- Attended National Marketing Society's "Wowing the Web Customer" conference
- Provided daily office functions for marketing department

Design Editor, *The State University Tribune*   2004–2005
- Designed inventive layout for weekly university newspaper that boosted ad sales 30 percent
- Managed design staff of three, handling hiring, budgeting, and training
- Converted design department from "SuperDesign" to "DesignPro 6.0"

Resident Assistant, State University   2003–2004
- Built and maintained dormitory Web site
- Led a dormitory hall of 30 residents
- Coordinated entertainment activities, and educational seminars
- Provided counseling and first aid services

Webmaster, Kappa Alpha Beta Sorority   2002–2005
- Redesigned and maintained sorority Web site, "KAB StateU.com"
- Web site won second place for "best sorority Web site" at KAB National Convention

---

This job seeker did some things to make this a strong "Experience" section. She doesn't list every detail of every activity—just what is relevant to this job (Web development, newspaper layout), as well as activities (resident assistant) that demonstrate overall maturity, a good work attitude, and other soft skills that would be valuable for any job. Use good judgment here, however. You may have been in the chess club or played a walk-on part in the school play, but those things don't relate to this particular job, so best to leave them off the "Experience" section.

Also note that this job seeker uses power words and makes mention of a Web design award she won.

Finally, she inserts numbers, demonstrating how she directly improved the bottom line for her university newspaper (her "inventive layout design boosted ad sales 30 percent").

What If Your Most Relevant Achievement for a Job Was Two Years Ago?

This is a very common quandary. Sometimes you'll find that your most important job-related experience was in work you did two years ago or more. If this is the case, you should still list your work experience chronologically, but if you have a particular experience that might give you a boost for a job, list it in a summary of qualifications (instead of the objective statement) at the top of your resume as well as in the Experience section, *and* be sure to highlight that experience in your cover letter.

For example, you are applying to work as a bank teller, and you were an assistant bookkeeper at a job two years ago. So, the summary of qualifications could look something like this:

Summary of Qualifications
- Assistant Bookkeeper, Fast-Care Minor Medical Center, 2003–2004
- Server, Wingers Sports Bar, Orlando, Fla., Summer 2005
- Salesperson, Foster Greenhouse, Orlando, Fla., Summer 2004

Another way to handle this situation is to create two sections for your experience—"Relevant Experience" and "Other Experience" to make your progression clear to the recruiter.

SKILLS

List your hard and soft skills here—especially the ones that relate to this job. Name specific software you are familiar with; don't just say "word processing," say "Microsoft Word." Also be sure to list any certifications you have earned, such as MCSE—these will definitely be keywords for technical positions.

Limit this section to skills that relate to the job in a concrete way—if you paint watercolors, this might relate to a graphic design job, but not to a bank teller position.

See the sample resume on page 116 for an example of well-executed "Skills" section.

EDUCATION

Here is where you list your institution, your degree, and the year of your graduation.

As mentioned earlier, if you attended a school considered top tier, or received a fellowship or award such as a Rhodes Scholarship, you should consider moving "Education" to the top of the resume, just beneath the objective statement.

Also be sure to list any "regular" educational awards you earned here, or higher on the resume if you feel they warrant such treatment—valedictorian, winner of school Creative Writing Contest, and so forth.

Do You List Your GPA?

Only if it's a good one—3.0 or higher. Or, if the job you are applying for requires it—many programs for new grads at investment banks, for example, only accept applicants with a certain minimum GPA. Most recruiters don't care if you leave it off altogether, so don't sweat it. You're in the real world now and it's your chance to start over—grades, good or bad, don't necessarily apply anymore.

hot facts •

Schools Recruiters Search for Most Frequently on Yahoo! HotJobs

1. Stanford	8. Princeton	15. Millersville
2. MIT	9. Brown	16. CMU
3. Harvard	10. Wharton	17. Suffolk
4. Columbia	11. NYU	18. Purdue
5. Berkeley	12. IIT	19. Nassau
6. Yale	13. Dartmouth	20. Colgate
7. Cornell	14. Duke	

What If You Changed Schools or Took More than Four Years to Graduate?

Again, don't sweat it. Just list the final school, degree, and the year you got it—the point is, you eventually *got* the degree.

▸ ▲ ◂
hot facts ●
▸ ▾ ◂

Degrees Recruiters Search for Most Frequently on Yahoo! HotJobs

1. Bachelor of Science
2. Bachelor of Arts
3. Bachelor of Business Administration
4. Master of Science
5. Associate's

6. Master of Business (MBA)
7. PhD
8. High School
9. Master of Arts
10. Juris Doctorate

Your Major

You may be asking yourself: Is my major really important? How crucial is it to my career in the grand scheme of things? The answer is . . . it depends.

Almost half (44 percent) of job seekers said that their major was "somewhat" relevant to the career they wanted to pursue, in a Yahoo! HotJobs' College Community survey. A third (36 percent) said it was "very" relevant. And a fifth (20 percent) said their major was "not at all" relevant.

In another poll, two-thirds of job seekers said that they currently work in a field unrelated to their college major. The remaining third were employed in a field that was related to their major.

The bottom line: If you chose the right major, you can use it to advance your career. And if you didn't choose so wisely, you can probably overcome it.

FINISHING TOUCHES: AWARDS AND HONORS, VOLUNTEER WORK, ACTIVITIES

The final sections of your resume offer a bit more flexibility, depending on your experiences.

"Awards and Honors" is where you can list notable awards you have won, but that don't necessarily apply to your job—State Judo Champion; Red Cross Volunteer of the Month. They simply demonstrate other aspects of your skills. If the award relates to the job, list it in the "Experience" section.

If you've done a lot of volunteer work, you might want to list it in a section titled **"Volunteer Work."** This applies to volunteer work you did on a semiregular basis—one-day commitments, occasional tutoring, and the like.

However, if that volunteer work involved more "working world" skills, and more of your time—for example, you managed a large project or were responsible for a major increase in donations—you will want to list it higher in the "Experience" section.

"Activities" is the section where you can list teams, clubs, and memberships in student or professional groups. These help demonstrate your well-roundedness and self-motivation, as well as depth of personality and additional skills. For example, you may enjoy teaching kids to swim, and it just so happens that the ad firm you are applying for is about to launch an ad campaign centered on getting kids to be more active. You never know.

However, avoid listing hobbies. They can rarely help your candidacy for a job and you may not be perceived as serious. If you're truly passionate about something, you can find a way to mention it in your interview. Interviewers often ask about outside interests, so you can share your hobbies there, in a more appropriate setting.

Also, be cautious when mentioning affiliations with political or religious groups, activist organizations, and the like, unless they are specifically related to the job for which you are applying (teaching at a religious school, for example). Be yourself, of course—you don't want to work in an environment in which your beliefs aren't respected or tolerated. But unless your affiliations relate to the work, or you earned a leadership position within a religious or political group, you should refrain from mentioning these facts on your resume.

A WORD ABOUT YOUR WORDS...

More than just your accomplishments make your resume stand out. How you communicate them matters, too.

For maximum impact, keep your resume as concise as you can. You need to include all your achievements in only one or two pages, so don't waste space on meaningless words. Power words such as "achieved," "created," and "implemented" give a clearer picture of what you did than words such as "helped" or "contributed."

Be specific—let an employer know the part you played and how you affected the outcome. Say exactly what you did in a previous position: "coded," "designed," "sold."

Also, don't flower your resume with fancy words. By trying to sound intelligent or qualified, you may end up annoying or confusing your reader. Avoid buzzwords that have become clichés and words that are unnecessarily sophisticated. "Synergy" and "liaise" are examples of buzzwords that have been overused and abused. Say what you mean plainly and simply. For example, instead of "interface," say "work." Instead of "impact," say "affect." Instead of "utilize," say "use." (See the sidebar below for more words to avoid.)

take a memo

Watch Your Words

Four phrases every resume should include:

- ☼ *Teamwork* or *team player:* more important in the workplace than ever
- ☼ *Detail-oriented:* shows you won't let things fall through the cracks
- ☼ *Self-motivated* or *self-starter:* you can generate your own ideas and follow them through to fruition
- ☼ *Flexible:* malleable employees who can "roll" with changes quickly are valuable

Words to avoid:

- ☼ **Abbreviations and acronyms** (unless they are universally recognized terms like BA, C++, or MCSE): Write out school names (State University, not "S.U.") and full names of volunteer organizations.
- ☼ **Personal pronouns:** Your resume is all about you; the addition of "I" or "me" is redundant.
- ☼ **Negative words:** Words such as *arrested, boring, failed,* and *fired* will catch recruiters' attention for the wrong reason. These terms refer to issues you can raise during the interview, if necessary.
- ☼ **Articles and abused words:** *a, also, an, because, the, very, successfully*—of course you performed a task successfully, or it wouldn't be on your resume in the first place!
- ☼ **Puffy words:** *panacea, revered.* Stick to formal but common language—get too flowery and you'll sound insincere.

SHOULD YOU USE A PROFESSIONAL RESUME WRITER?

For an entry-level job seeker, retaining a professional resume writer is likely an expense you can't take on.

However, if you would feel better with a pro, select one affiliated with a reputable company with a proven track record, such as ResumeEdge (http://hotjobs.resumeedge.com). Or look for someone who is a member of a professional resume writers association, such as the Professional Association of Resume Writers & Career Coaches (PARW/CC).

OTHER STICKY QUESTIONS

What if my resume doesn't take up a full page? You're not the first one to contend with that problem. You can use some word processing tricks—widening the margins, enlarging the font—but don't go overboard. Recruiters realize that you're just entering the workforce. Do the best you can and in the meantime get out there and create more experiences for yourself through volunteering, part-time work, and internships.

Is it OK to "fudge" things on a resume? No, no, and no. With the background and reference checks routinely performed today, a white lie can catch up with you—even if it's several years down the road. The truth always has a way of getting out.

Take a lesson from these famous downfalls:

- In 2004, James Minder, CEO of Smith & Wesson Holding Corp., resigned after it was revealed that he had served fifteen years in prison for several armed robberies.

- In 2002, Quincy Troupe, California's first poet laureate, stepped down after a background check showed that he hadn't graduated from college as he'd claimed.

- In 2001, Coach George O'Leary resigned from Notre Dame's football program just days after joining. Having claimed he'd earned a master's degree in education and played college football for three years, O'Leary admitted it wasn't true.

What if I quit or was fired from a job, internship, or team? Everyone makes mistakes, but being fired doesn't look so good in black and white. Consider listing the experience without listing the outcome. Or, leave it off altogether. Be prepared to explain in an interview why you left the job, if asked.

Emma Philip

123 Heritage Lane ◆ Anytown, USA 55555
555-555-5555 ◆ emma_philip2001@yahoo.com

OBJECTIVE

To use my Web development skills to build exciting, informative Web sites in the nonprofit industry.

EXPERIENCE

Developed award-winning Web sites for university, community and commercial organizations.

Intern, Happy Cola Marketing Department, Atlanta, Georgia   Spring 2005
- Learned advanced Web development with award-winning Web design team for nation's No. 2 soft drink producer
- Coded HTML for "Intern Info," an intranet site for Happy Cola interns
- Attended National Marketing Society's "Wowing the Web Customer" conference
- Provided daily office functions for marketing department

Design Editor, *The State University Tribune*   2004–2005
- Designed inventive layout for weekly university newspaper that boosted ad sales 30%
- Managed design staff of three, including hiring, budgeting and training
- Converted design department from "SuperDesign" to "DesignPro 6.0"

Resident Assistant, State University   2003–2004
- Built and maintained dormitory Web site
- Led dormitory hall of 30 residents
- Coordinated entertainment, activities, and educational seminars
- Provided counseling and first aid services

Webmaster, Kappa Alpha Beta Sorority   2002–2005
- Redesigned and maintained sorority Web site, "KABStateU.com"
- Web site won second place for "best sorority Web site" at KAB National Convention

SKILLS

Microsoft Office, Quark, Adobe Illustrator, DreamWeaver, Homesite, American Sign Language.

EDUCATION

B.S., Computer Science, State University (3.7 GPA)
University of London Study-Abroad Program, Spring 2003, London, England

VOLUNTEER WORK

Webmaster, Red Cross, Anytown Chapter   2004
- Served food at temporary shelter following Hurricane Charlie
- Coordinated State University fall semester blood drive

ACTIVITIES

- President, Future Designers of America, State University Chapter
- Member, Anytown League of Web Developers

Do I include references? Not on the resume. If a job asks for references, supply them on a separate sheet. It's fairly common at the bottom of the resume to include a header for "References" and underneath state "Available upon request." (See page 138 for more on references.)

What if the job asks for my salary requirements? There's a general rule not to mention salary before an interview, since your desired salary may put you out of the running. However, if specifically asked, you need to put something down. First things first: Where do you put it? If necessary, always specify salary requirements in the cover letter, never in the resume. Second, what do you put down? If you're feeling flexible, you could write "negotiable." This should at least prevent you from being excluded from the first round of consideration. If you do have a salary requirement, as a result of student loans, rent, or car payments, then consider listing a range.

Remember, your resume should be a living, breathing document. It's not a once-a-year type of thing. Revisit it frequently. Add to your resume as you obtain new skills and experiences.

Recommended Books

Resumes for Dummies by Joyce Lain Kennedy (John Wiley & Sons, ISBN 0764554719, $16.99).

Resumes That Knock 'em Dead (Knock 'em Dead Series) by Martin Yate (Adams Media Corporation, ISBN 159337108X, $12.95).

Damn Good Resume Guide: A Crash Course in Resume Writing by Yana Parker (Ten Speed Press, ISBN 1580084443, $9.95).

Your First Resume: For Students and Anyone Preparing to Enter Today's Tough Job Market by Ron Fry (Delmar Learning, ISBN 1564145832, $11.99).

Best Resumes for College Students and New Grads: Jump-Start Your Career! by Louise M. Kursmark (JIST Works, Inc., ISBN 1563709007, $12.95).

The Dog Ate My Resume: Survival Tips for Life after College, by Zack Arnstein & Larry Arnstein (Santa Monica Press, ISBN 189166137X, $11.95).

Recommended Web Sites

Yahoo! HotJobs—Resume Writing:
http://hotjobs.yahoo.com/resume

Rockport Institute's How to Write a Masterpiece of a Resume:
www.rockportinstitute.com/resumes.html

ResumeEdge:
http://hotjobs.resumeedge.com

ResumeTutor:
www.umn.edu/ohr/ecep/resume

Online Writing Lab's Resume Writing Workshop:
http://owl.english.purdue.edu/workshops/hypertext/ResumeW

Loyola University Chicago's Guide for Writing Effective Resumes
www.luc.edu/resources/career/resguide.pdf

7-Step Resume Sampler:
www.7step-resumesampler.com/step1.html

CHAPTER 9

So, Tell Me About Yourself: Mastering the Interview

"Come. Sit. Speak."

t's truly one of the most agonizing parts of the job-seeking process—
wondering if you'll get a chance to interview for that great job for which you
just applied!

Days go by, and nothing. Then, after what seems like years of waiting, the
phone rings. You answer, heart racing, hand trembling. On the other end is the
recruiter with the news you've been so longing to hear:

"Hi Kelly. This is Sean with Acme, Inc. We've reviewed your resume and feel
you could be a great candidate. We'd like you to come in for an interview—are
you available next week?"

Of course you are! But then you hang up and feel a surge of anxiety, that stab
of adrenaline in your chest that comes from your doubts:

*What do I say? What will I wear? What if I don't get the job? What if I don't
get any job ever and I'm stuck living at home in the basement for the rest of my
life, then die a lonely, jobless death and no one even knows to look for me?*

Stop right there. The interview isn't a circus act in which you're the lion and
the interviewer is the ringmaster, cracking a whip and forcing you to leap through
flaming hoops (although it may feel that way).

The interview is a conversation in which you and the employer can get to know
each other and find out whether or not you are a good fit for each other's needs.

In this chapter, we'll take a look at the interview process. We'll discuss the
people you'll meet, what they're looking for, how to present your qualifications,
the questions you might be asked, even what to wear—all the important things
you'll need to remember to help you make a great impression and hopefully
land a job.

"HI. NICE TO MEET YOU. I HOLD YOUR TINY FUTURE IN MY HANDS"

You'll encounter several people as you undergo the interview process—and you
should be professional and polite to all of them as each may or may not be con-
tacted for feedback about you. (We looked at these roles briefly in chapter 2.)

The Receptionist: This will likely be the first person you encounter as you
wait for the HR person or hiring manager to come for you. You should be polite
to her, of course, and remember that the interview begins as soon as you walk
in the door.

HR Representative/Recruiter: At last you match a face to the voice on the
phone. The HR representative or recruiter will likely meet you for a preliminary
screen and paperwork before your interview.

Hiring Manager: This is the person you'll want to impress the most because she will not only be your main interviewer, but also—if you get the job—your boss.

The Hiring Manager's Direct Report: Sometimes, due to schedule changes, a hiring manager will farm out the job of interviewing to someone secondary to him. In this case, you should consider it your main priority to impress this interviewer.

The Hiring Manager's Manager: This is your would-be boss' boss. However, while you certainly want to put your best foot forward with this one, and she will have some input, it's still the hiring manager who will ultimately make the call on whether or not you're hired.

Potential Coworkers: You may meet or even be interviewed by one or more people with whom you will work if you are hired. You might be tempted to let your guard down with the guy who is your age and also a Red Sox fan, or the woman who wore jeans to work today. Don't do it—maintain professionalism at all times, no matter who you are talking to during the interview.

TYPES OF INTERVIEWS

Just as there is no one type of position or company, there is also no one type of interview.

Traditional

In a traditional interview, you'll come to the company and meet with the hiring manager for probably a half-hour or longer. You'll discuss your work history and experience, education, and the reasons you're interested in the company. You'll find out about company culture, the team you could potentially work with, and possibly compensation.

Phone Interviews/Screenings

Be aware that sometimes the recruiter's call itself may be an initial interview. Treat it as if it were a formal interview. Take the call someplace quiet—if you need to call the recruiter back later, do so.

Group Interviews

As if one person to impress isn't enough, sometimes you'll be asked to interview with two or more people at the same time.

But don't see it as being "ganged-up on"; rather, consider it an opportunity to impress several people at once!

take a memo

Phone Interview Tips

Although on the phone you might feel safer with some distance between you and your interviewer, you still should be just as professional as if the person were in the same room with you.

- ☼ Find a quiet place to take the call, away from the computer, the TV, loud roommates, family dogs, or other distractions.

- ☼ If it's not a good time to talk, say so—the recruiter will understand. Tell him how pleased you are that he called, confirm his callback number, and then reschedule for a time (soon) when you are better prepared.

- ☼ Have your resume and a pen and paper handy.

- ☼ Be positive and enthusiastic—try to smile while you're talking. Interviewers can hear it in your voice, and it will boost your mood and calm your nerves.

- ☼ Stand up—this will make you feel more confident.

- ☼ Listen carefully to your interviewer's questions, and his or her responses to your answers.

- ☼ Have some questions prepared for the inevitable, "Do you have any questions?"

- ☼ Practice a phone interview with a friend ahead of time.

To impress multiple interviewers, make eye contact with both the individual asking the question and the group as a whole. Smile and try to connect topics to the people who asked about them. Don't interrupt. *Interesting fact:* In some countries, it's common for the interviewer to meet with multiple candidates at once.

Case-Based Interviews

In certain professions like finance and consulting, you may be given a real-life business problem and asked to form a plan for solving it. To prepare, you can read sample case studies of companies online, or speak with one of your college business professors about the latest trends of which you need to be aware.

Meal Interviews

Meal interviews may seem less formal than office interviews, but they are just as important. Some tips:

- ☼ Brush up on basic table manners—for examples, scan the definitive book on the subject, *Emily Post's Etiquette*.

- ☼ Avoid messy foods like burgers or spaghetti and do not order alcohol, even if your interviewer does—you want to be clear-headed. Order a medium-priced item and no dessert. If you're uncertain how to behave, follow the interviewer's lead.

- ☼ Have a snack beforehand—that way, you won't be hungry going into the meal. You'll feel better as the interview begins, and more alert as you're talking about your background.

- ☼ Don't offer to pay for the meal—it's not expected. Don't ask for a doggy bag either.

Pre-Employment Tests

While not interviews themselves, some jobs will require writing, software, or even personality tests. These can take up to several hours; the recruiter may give you the choice of scheduling them on a day other than your interview. Do whatever you feel will allow you to perform your best at both.

PREPPING FOR AN INTERVIEW

As you prep for an interview, use your research on the job, the hiring manager, and the company to present yourself as the type of candidate who would fit in there. Remember that the way you come across will largely be unspoken. Your attire, punctuality (or lack thereof), and general demeanor may say more about you than your words.

You Are What You Wear

Many first-time job seekers struggle with what would seem to be a simple decision—what to wear to an interview. Today, as khakis and sneakers have pushed aside wool and linen in many workplaces, it's easy to see why this would be confusing.

Professional attire, even if you are applying for a job that doesn't require it, is key. Why? Because your clothes give hints about who you are. Will a man who insists on wearing jeans among others in suits be a team player? Maybe

take a memo

Recruiter Cheat Sheet: Interviewing

Don't go to your interview without first reading these tips from Amy Costa, Specialty Recruiting Manager, BearingPoint:

Early bird gets the worm. Always arrive at least fifteen minutes early to your interview to get settled in at the reception desk and have a couple of minutes to prepare.

Preparation is key. Remember to research the company before your interview. Know key facts about company culture, history, and financials.

Think before you speak. Take a moment to reflect before answering a question, and articulate a clear, concise answer rather than rambling on.

Grand finale. Always ask the interviewer for a business card, and verify that the e-mail address is included.

Always mind your "pleases" and "thank-yous." Ask, "May I please have your business card?" and remember to say, "Thank you for your time" at the end of the interview. Follow up with a formal thank-you note.

Dress for success. Even if the company has a casual dress code, it is always better to be over- than underdressed.

Interview the interviewer. Prepare thought-provoking questions to ask the interviewer.

Take note. Bring a notebook or a pad of paper to take notes (this will help you personalize your thank-you note later).

so, but the clothes don't reflect that. Does a woman whose skirt is wrinkled pay attention to details? Maybe, but unconsciously she's sending a message that she does not.

Dress conservatively, and don't wear excessive jewelry, makeup, perfume, or cologne. Men should wear a suit; women should wear a long skirt, pants, or a pantsuit, and conservative, closed-toe shoes. Suits in conservative colors, such as black and navy, are a safe choice for both men and women. Wear them with a white or solid-colored shirt for a tasteful, professional look—avoid wild patterns or extreme colors. (Unsure? Black is always a good choice.) Both men and women should avoid casual shoes and "golf" shirts; turtlenecks are not advisable for men.

Feel too stiff in a suit? Reconsider. In fact, Susan Bixler, president of The Professional Image, Inc., recommends always wearing a jacket—this gives you a serious, professional appearance.

▶ ▲ ◀
hot facts •
▶ ▼ ◀
Dress for Success

Interview attire can have an effect on your eventual salary offer. Research suggests that the right interview outfit can increase your salary between 8 and 20 percent, according to Susan Bixler, president of the corporate image consulting firm The Professional Image, Inc. (www.theprofessional image.net). An interviewer will believe that the way you look at the interview is the best you can do. What you wear makes a statement—make it a good one.

Tank tops, midriff shirts, and skirts more than one or two inches above the knee are absolutely a no-no, as well as tight-fitting clothing, no matter how conservative.

Be sure your shoes are polished. Hair should be clean and neat—it's time to get rid of the blue streaks if you want to be taken seriously in the working world. Same for tattoos and body piercings—if you have them, conceal them. In fact, 90 percent of job seekers said that tattoos or piercings could cost them a job in a survey in Yahoo! HotJobs' College Community. If you want to use your attire to express your individuality, do so in a *small, subtle* way. Women can wear a piece of tasteful jewelry, and men can sport an elegant tie.

Finally, make sure nails are trimmed and clean, and ladies: no purple polish, excessive length, or airbrush designs.

As an entry-level job seeker, your budget is probably pretty tight. Invest in one good interview outfit—for women, a skirt or pantsuit; for men, a good, tailored suit (ill-fitting clothing suggests that you might be sloppy in your work). In addition, consider borrowing clothing items from like-sized friends. Find quality shirts in solid colors that don't require dry cleaning. Shop at vintage, consignment, or charity shops for great suit bargains.

Details Count

Now that you've figured out what to wear, here are some easier tips to remember:

Be fifteen minutes early. Any more and you look overeager; any less and you are cutting it too close. Allow for traffic jams, the absence of parking spaces, and getting lost or otherwise delayed. Carry the recruiter's phone number with you in case you get unavoidably detained, and if you will be late, be sure to call and let him know.

Shake hands. A firm handshake is a must, whether you are a man or woman and whether the employer is a man or woman. A University of Alabama study found that a person's handshake reflects certain key personality traits, including confidence, degree of shyness, and neuroticism. (Not surprisingly, folks with firmer handshakes were found to be more confident, less shy, and less neurotic.)

Leave your cell phone off or in the car. This bears repeating. Turn your cell phone off or leave it in the car.

What to Bring

You don't need the latest designer briefcase for an interview. You *will* need:

- Several copies of your resume on quality paper. Don't assume that just because you have already e-mailed it to the recruiter she will have it.
- Copies of your references. These should consist of at least three people, be listed on a separate sheet of paper from your resume, and list the names, titles, addresses, phone numbers, and e-mail addresses of each, if possible.
- If the job warrants, samples of your best work to share.
- A notebook and a pen.
- A "cheat sheet" of your elevator speech and top skills to glance at before or even as you interview.
- Business cards if you have them.
- A basic case, leather binder, or plain leather satchel to carry the items— *no backpacks.*
- Have your items at the ready. Digging through your purse for a pen is distracting.

▶**Action Items: Pre-Interview Prep**

As you prepare, try the following pre-interview techniques:

- Have you ever interviewed anyone before—for a summer job, dog sitting, lawn mowing? Think back to that experience. What impressed you about someone you interviewed? What qualities did you look for? If you've never interviewed someone, imagine what qualities and skills you would seek.
- Do a mock interview with a friend. What nervous tics do they notice about you? What questions do you struggle with?
- Write out answers to the most difficult questions on flash cards. Study the cards and carry them to interviews for last-minute prep.

THE INNER WORKINGS OF THE INTERVIEW

Every interview is unique, but generally it will break down into three parts: introductions and small talk, discussion/evaluation of your qualifications and personality, and wrapping things up.

We'll discuss each of these elements in detail; but, first, it's important to understand what goals you and the interviewer are trying to achieve during the interview process.

A Hiring Manager's Goals in an Interview

You may think the interviewer is sizing you up, searching out your every flaw, noting your every mistake. But, in fact, a hiring manager is looking for a wider range of characteristics than whether or not you have broccoli stuck in your teeth. She is trying to answer three fundamental questions:

1. Is this person qualified for the job?
2. Will this person fit into our culture?
3. How can this individual help solve a particular problem?

Think of interviewing with a "big picture" perspective. When you get nervous, remember that there is more she is looking for than the perfect answers to her questions—being professional and positive are just as important.

Your Goals in an Interview

An interview is also a chance for you to learn more about the employer and the position. There are five things you need to do to accomplish that:

1. *Establish rapport:* Create a comfortable interviewing environment by being open, sincere, personable, having positive body language, and being professional, but approachable.

2. *Sell yourself:* Get across your main selling points and highlight your biggest achievements. Let the interviewer know that you understand the job for which you are applying by relating its needs to your experience.

3. *Listen:* Listen to what the interviewer says and take notes. Be prepared for the interviewer to take the driver's seat. Do not interrupt.

4. *Ask questions:* Usually, the interviewer will let you know when it's time to ask questions. Be sure you have some ready. It shows that you are proactive. But, remember, some questions are better suited for the recruiter and some for the employer. (See page 25.)

5. *Get next steps/feedback:* Don't leave an interview not knowing what to do next. Clarify with the interviewer what the follow-up process will be.

At the end of an interview an employer should know whether she wants your candidacy to proceed, and you should know whether you still want to proceed. Sometimes you'll find that a job is everything you wanted and more—and therefore you may need to do more practicing and research to be ready for a second interview or offer if it comes. Or you may realize that a job is not suited for you—and that's okay too. As we said, that is what an interview is for.

INTRODUCTIONS AND SMALL TALK

You'll probably first be met in the lobby by a human resources representative—quite possibly the recruiter with whom you've spoken. She'll escort you to her office or a conference room for an initial screening, and possibly give you some additional paperwork to fill out.

It's important to remember that your interview actually begins the moment you walk in the door and continues as you walk down the hallway to the interviewer's office. How you conduct yourself in the first few minutes is just as important as how you act during the actual interview.

As you meet your various interviewers, remember that the "little things"—your body language, confidence, and handshake—will say as much about you as your actual words (if not more). Maintain eye contact, and remind yourself that they asked you to come here today—you deserve this job! Shake hands firmly, and emanate a positive attitude.

Remember that small talk is not so small after all. Even in the first five minutes of meeting a recruiter or an employer, he is already making an impression of you—good small talk can begin creating positive impressions of you in others' minds—as can bad small talk. Don't discuss how bad the traffic was on the way to the interview or how late you were out the night before. Instead, be upbeat and try to mention something positive about something as simple as the weather, or, better yet, an article you saw in the newspaper that morning about the company or industry.

DISCUSSION

The recruiter may go over points on your resume and review the qualifications for the job. In some cases, the recruiter will be the only person who will interview you that day, and if all goes well, have you come back again later to meet the hiring manager. If this is the case, the recruiter—whose daily job involves working with job applicants—will likely ask you different questions than the hiring manager will. The recruiter might ask broader questions that involve the company as a whole, whereas the hiring manager is more focused on finding out information about you and your skills as they relate to his department. As we discussed in chapter 2, your questions for these two individuals should differ. Questions about benefits, salary, and company culture are best asked of the recruiter. The hiring manager can answer questions about the daily duties, the team, growth opportunities within the department, and so on.

Job Qualifications

Once you're past the small talk, it's time for the meat of the interview—the discussion of your qualifications.

Whether you're meeting with the recruiter or the hiring manager, first and foremost, the interviewer is most interested in whether or not you are qualified for the job. He may ask questions like, "So, why do you want to work at Acme, Inc.?" or "What made you apply for this position?" If you're currently employed, he will likely ask you why you want to leave your current position.

He'll also ask questions that get at the heart of your resume. He'll want to know about the background you have listed, as well as other experience not on your resume. He will probably ask you for more detail on those most interesting and relevant parts, as well as any perceived gaps in your experience, or skills the job requires that you may be lacking.

For example:

"What was the most enjoyable part of your last part-time job? The least?"

"How do you feel your college education prepared you for the workforce?"

"You're skilled in Software Design 4.2. Have you had much experience with Design Pro 3.1?"

Listen carefully to the questions and don't be afraid to ask for clarification if necessary. Use keywords from the job ad as you answer, and always relate your skills and experience to the job.

For example, let's say Jane is applying to work in the community outreach department of a large company. The job ad asks for "creativity" and a "goal-oriented" person to assist nonprofit organizations in the community with "fund-raising." She is asked, "What makes you qualified to apply for this position?" and responds:

"You'll see on my resume that I founded State University's chapter of Big Brothers/Big Sisters. This involved using creative methods of fund-raising to reach our goals—something about which I was very driven. For example, I organ-ized a carnival on campus to raise money and introduce the kids to potential Big Brothers and Sisters . . ."

Other questions for this portion of the interview could be:

"How have you used Quark in past positions?"

"I see you wrote for the school newspaper. How else have you used your communication skills?"

"What other volunteer work have you done and did you accomplish your goals?"

As you discuss your background, feel free to elaborate on key points from your resume, or even those not listed. Keep your successes and elevator speech in mind as you formulate answers to these questions.

Your Personality

An interviewer will want to find out more about your personality and passion for the job. He'll ask such questions as "What do you like most about volunteering?" or "What has been the most challenging situation you have had to handle and how did you resolve it?" Such questions aim to get at your attitude and work ethic.

There is no wrong answer as long as you are upbeat and show that you are capable of learning from difficult situations. In fact, this portion of the interview allows you the most freedom in your answers. Take advantage of this chance to mention successes that haven't yet been discussed. For example:

"I ran my first marathon this year and finished nine minutes under my goal time. I accomplished this by dedicated daily training and time management."

"As captain of my college debate team, I led us from the bottom of the rankings to the championship my senior year."

"I enjoy volunteering because not only has it taught me skills I can use in the business world, but it also helps me keep things in perspective."

While you obviously want to establish a rapport with the interviewer, try to steer your answers back to the job whenever possible. For example, Eric, apply-ing for an entry-level marketing position, had come prepared with experiences and skills he was eager to share with the hiring manager. He was surprised and initially pleased when they ended up discussing their mutual interest in sports for a good portion of the interview. Eric thought they had clicked, and looked forward to receiving an offer. Yet he never heard back from the company. What may have happened is that the hiring manager, most likely an inexperienced interviewer, was more impressed by another candidate who was able to work her relevant experience into the conversation. The hiring manager never got to find out just how qualified Eric was for the position.

Company Culture

The interviewer will also want to see how you'd fit into the company culture. Questions that delve into that include:

"Do you like to work as part of a team or alone?"

"How do you handle disagreement or conflict?"

"How do you feel about working weekends?"

"Do you prefer frequent contact and feedback with a manager, or more independence?"

Remember not to get defensive, and be honest with yourself about what you need from company culture. Don't say that you can work on a PR campaign to build a highway through protected forest if you believe strongly in protecting the environment. If you have something you want to say but the opportunity has not come up yet, by all means, segue (carefully) into this topic during the conversation:

"I'd like to add to your question earlier about teamwork. I mentioned my experiences as activities coordinator of a local teen center. Last year, the teens and I volunteered at the annual Anytown Food Drive, in which we coordinated the donations for the east side of Anytown—roughly 5,000 people. We collected $4,000 in food and donations."

You're Up!

After the interviewer has asked his questions, he may ask you for yours. You'll impress him if you have prepared "real" questions that go beyond "Where will I sit?" Your questions will depend on whom you're asking.

Questions for the Recruiter

☼ "Hiring here at Acme has increased by 20 percent in the last six months. Is this due to the pending acquisition of ABC Corp.?"

☼ "Acme has been ranked by *Working Woman* Magazine as being one of the top 100 companies for women. What makes your culture so female-friendly?"

☼ "What are the next steps in the hiring process?"

Questions for the Hiring Manager

- ☼ "What's the ideal candidate for this position like?"

- ☼ "What can I expect in terms of growth opportunities with this position?"

- ☼ "Acme recently was named by the *Wall Street Journal* as one of the twenty up-and-coming companies in the U.S. How does this department contribute to Acme's success?"

- ☼ "How do you measure success at Acme, Inc.?"

FACING THE TOUGH QUESTIONS

There are some universal stumpers that often come up at interviews—here are some of the biggest ones and some sample answers:

"Tell Me a Little about Yourself."

Sometimes the most general question can be the hardest. How can you sum up your entire life story in just a couple of minutes?

You don't. This is not a question about your hobbies or your family. Instead, it's a request for you to describe what you can offer the company.

In his excellent book *101 Great Answers to the Toughest Interview Questions*, author Ron Fry suggests focusing on:

- ☼ Your key accomplishments at previous jobs

- ☼ The strengths demonstrated by those accomplishments

- ☼ How these relate to the job for which you're applying

The goal is not to summarize your resume—the interviewer already has a copy of that. Rather, explain how you came to be interested in this particular company and job, and weave examples of past accomplishments throughout to demonstrate why you are the perfect candidate.

"What Is Your Biggest Weakness?"

Don't answer with "I'm always late" or "I get bored really easily." These are controllable choices that should be altered before you enter the workforce. And don't overcompensate with insincere answers: "I am a workaholic—I love long hours" or "Vacations are for wusses." The interviewer will see right through that.

THINK Outside the Box

Hello? Anyone There?

Sometimes you'll face an interviewer who either doesn't know, or doesn't care, to ask the right questions. This leaves you struggling not only to get across your strong points, but also to find out what you need to know about the job.

Start by asking some informal questions to break the ice, such as:

"I see you have some pictures from Walt Disney World on your desk. I just got back. Did you try the new Shrek ride?"

"I've read that many employees in your company do volunteer work— do they perform that work as individuals or do they work together to have a larger impact?"

If you are the one steering the interview, you might as well use the situation to your advantage. Highlight all your strong points and relate them to what you know about the company: "You asked if I would like working in finance. Yes, in college I was an economics major and enjoyed my math classes most."

Ask questions that will flatter the interviewer and draw her out of her shell. For example: "Your department has increased sales by 20 percent. That's impressive. How did you accomplish this?"

The "weakness" question is popular with interviewers not because they want to torture you, but because they're interested in hearing how you tackle challenges. So name a weakness, and then turn it around so that your conquering of it makes you look like a motivated problem solver. Also, pick a weakness that is real, but understandable or relatively benign. Whatever weakness you pick, be sure that it is work-related.

Here are a few examples:

☼ "I used to have a tendency to procrastinate. So now I am always sure to set a strict schedule for all my projects well in advance and I set personal deadlines. This organization has really helped."

☼ "Once in a while, I focus too much on the details of a project. So now, when I'm working on a project, I always make sure at the end of the day to sit back and take a few minutes to think about the general scope of my work. It forces me to keep priorities straight and helps me keep the right mind-set."

☼ "I used to have some problems with organization. So now I carry a schedule book around throughout the day and I also use my Palm Pilot to keep me on track. It's worked out great!"

You don't want to pick a weakness that will torpedo your chances—even your weakness should speak strongly about your skills.

"Where Do You See Yourself in Five Years?"

No, you don't have to say, "Right here at Acme." Instead, the best tactic: Talk about your values.

Don't get too detailed about your specific career plan. Instead, discuss things that are important to you professionally and how you plan to achieve them. If growth is a goal, mention that. You can also talk about challenge, another value that employers prize in their employees:

☼ "I would relish the opportunity to be part of the team preparing for such an important product launch. I think the aggressive timeline would be very energizing."

☼ "I see myself working at a hospital that values patient care over bureaucracy."

☼ "In five years, I'd like to be a manager of a team of artists and developers who seek to create exciting Web sites with the user in mind, not just the product."

"Why Should We Hire You?"

There's a fine line between boastful and confident and you need to learn it.

When an interviewer asks you why she should hire you, you're going to have to speak confidently and honestly about your abilities:

☼ "I believe the combination of my art history degree and my summers spent working at the Smith Gallery give me the experience you're looking for to boost attendance at this museum."

☼ "You mentioned that you would like to launch your new soda by the end of the year. During my experience interning at ABC Marketing, I wrote copy for the company Web site for a similar, successful product launch."

Aim for earnest and prepare by practicing. That's right: Stand in front of the mirror and acknowledge your abilities and accomplishments to your reflection. Tell yourself: I have a very strong work ethic. I have integrity. I have excellent industry contacts. I aggressively pursue my goals.

It's sometimes hard to praise yourself, but after a few sessions you'll sound sincere.

INAPPROPRIATE INTERVIEW QUESTIONS

Inappropriate interview questions generally involve race, sex, religion, national origin, or age.

Some examples:

"How old are you?"
"Now that you've graduated, any plans to settle down and start a family?"
"Who will take care of your kids while you're at work?"
"What country are you from?"
"So, you got a boyfriend?"

Making a hiring decision based on the answers to these questions is illegal and, therefore, they should not come up in an interview. But, if they do, you have three options for handling them.

Answer the Question

If you're comfortable providing the information, go ahead and do it so the interview can proceed. However, only offer the requested information if you are truly comfortable giving it. Otherwise, you're setting a precedent that you're accepting of inappropriate behavior.

Refuse to Answer the Question

Calmly tell the interviewer that the question doesn't seem relevant to the interview or the job's requirements. Save such a direct response, however, for questions that are offensive or deeply troubling—in other words, questions that bother you enough to make you reconsider the job.

Don't Answer the Question, but Answer the Question *Behind* the Question

This is usually the best option, because it allows you to provide a tactful answer without sacrificing your rights. Try to figure out what the interviewer *really* wants to know.

For example, say an interviewer has asked if you are a U.S. citizen (which is an inappropriate question). Rephrase the question into an appropriate one and then answer it—for example, "If you mean to ask if I am legally authorized to work in the United States, the answer is yes."

Be careful what you divulge in an interview about your personal life, whether you are asked or not. If you plan to get married soon, are pregnant or soon to become pregnant, have an illness or disability, do not mention this in an interview—you are not obligated to do so. (Also, be wary of mentioning any blogs you maintain.)

If you have concerns or questions about inappropriate interview questions, visit the Equal Employment Opportunity Commission Web site at www.eeoc.gov.

WHAT NOT TO SAY IN AN INTERVIEW

An interview can be incredibly stressful—sometimes you'll find yourself grasping for words. Always keep the following in mind:

Skip the "filler." When an interviewer asks a question, you may feel as if you need to rush into an answer. Or you may lose track of your thoughts and stall with "ya know" or "ummm." Taking time to think about a question, rather than rushing to answer, can help eliminate the need to use filler. If you need a moment to think, say so—that's perfectly acceptable.

Don't jargon your way out of a job. Avoid such words and acronyms as "synergy," "ROI," and the like. You may think jargon makes you sound knowledgeable, but it can appear transparent—especially if the interviewer doesn't know the terms. Speak simply and coherently; your intelligence should speak for itself.

Why slang is "way bad." Slang—"wassup," "chillin,' "—sounds unprofessional, even immature. Speak to an interviewer just as you would to a business colleague or even a boss. And never, ever, use profanity in an interview. There's simply no place for it.

Don't answer before you've been asked. First, it's rude to interrupt. Second, you may incorrectly assume that you know what the interviewer was going to ask and answer the wrong question. Third, you won't have time to think about your

take a memo

Salary

Although salary may not come up in the first interview, sooner or later you will have to have that discussion—most likely with the recruiter first. He may ask for your requirements, in which case you can give several answers—but not a hard number. Why? If your number is too low, you might get paid less than what you are worth; too high and you can self-select yourself out of the running. Instead, give answers with ranges:

- ☼ "From my research I see that advertising firms in this region pay $30,000 to $40,000 for a position like this one."
- ☼ "I'd like to learn more about this position first, and I know you'd like to know more about me as well."
- ☼ "I'd like to give this position some consideration first and perhaps call you with further questions. May we table the salary discussion until another time?"
- ☼ "What is the established range for this position?"

Another alternative is to give your salary range and, if the recruiter pushes back, say that you're open to discussing other forms of compensation (more vacation time, a signing bonus, and the like).

Salary and benefits are a large, important topic we'll discuss further in chapter 10.

---

answer before you start speaking, which can lead to midsentence "ummms" to stall for time.

When an interviewer asks a question, it's tempting to answer quickly, especially if you're nervous. Don't. Instead, wait for her to finish speaking, then take a deep breath and collect your thoughts. Then answer the question. You'll appear calm, confident, and polite. And, after taking a moment to think, you'll probably give a much better answer too.

WRAPPING UP

As the interview comes to a close, the interviewer will begin to ask you for your final thoughts and questions. From there you'll either be finished or escorted to speak with others—the employer's boss or other employees, in which case you need simply to follow the same approach as with the interviewer—be polite, professional, ask questions, and listen.

Remember that the interviewer might well be meeting another candidate right after you—so you want to leave her with an excellent impression.

Be confident and reiterate your interest in the position. Use the final few minutes of your job interview to emphasize the skills that make you right for the job. This will ensure that your strengths will be one of the last things that the interviewer hears—helping her to remember them.

Rehearse your closing so that you are not fumbling over your words. You'll want to sound smooth and natural, not boastful. Start by saying how impressed you are with the company and the people you've met. Then transition into why you'd be a good fit for the position. Ask the interviewer if there's anything else you can do to show your strengths as a candidate. For example, you can offer to send samples of your work, if appropriate.

Now is also your chance to show you have been listening and that you understand what the job requires. Try to ask one last question, or make a final, definitive statement about yourself. For example:

> *"You mentioned that Acme hopes to boost sales by 25 percent this year. What plans do you have to revise your current retail strategy to meet that goal?"*

Or,

> *"I believe my retail management experience over the last year can help Acme increase its sales by 25 percent this year, as you mentioned."*

Or,

> *"I really enjoyed meeting you. I feel my biology degree and experience volunteering at the local hospital could help me be an asset to your company."*

REFERENCES

As the interview wraps up, you should also be prepared for the interviewer to ask you for references. Have your list of three up-to-date references with their contact information handy. Consider using college professors, especially those who know your work and have a high opinion of you; previous employers; and student government leaders. You should be sure each one knows you will be using him or her as a reference and that the reference will indeed say good things about you.

Outside the Box

Five Ways to Rescue a Dying Interview

Although anyone can make an overt mistake in an interview, sometimes interviews fizzle for no apparent reason. Here are some things you can do to get things back on track:

1. Smile. A big grin will help relax you and the interviewer.

2. Turn the tables. If you feel that you just aren't giving the right answers to an interviewer's questions, try changing tactics—and ask the interviewer a few questions of your own:

What's your favorite thing about working here?
What's a typical day like working in this department?

If you momentarily switch the focus from yourself to the interviewer, it will give you a chance to regroup and compose yourself. Also, it will make the interviewer do some talking, perhaps giving you a clue to what he is looking for.

3. Ask for clarification. If your interviewer seems bored or confused by your answer to a question, stop and ask if you are giving him the information he requested.

4. Give a compliment. More specifically, give a compliment to the company. State how friendly everyone is or how nice the view is from the interviewer's window. This will show that you are a positive person without sounding insincere.

5. Do your best and move on. Maybe the discomfort is not your fault—maybe the interviewer is having a bad day or is just not that good at his job. Trust yourself and don't worry about things you can't control.

Remember that crotchety economics professor? He might not be the best reference for you—or anyone else.

FOLLOW-UP

Waiting to hear the decision on a position is tough enough—don't leave a job interview without knowing the next step in the hiring process.

For example: Will there be another round of interviews? When do they anticipate that a decision will be made? How will you find out the results—will someone call you or will you receive a letter? You may also want to ask the recruiter how he would prefer you to follow up with him. Can you call him, or would he rather that you email him? Not only will this information help reduce post-interview anxiety, it also shows the interviewer that you're thorough and conscientious.

THANK-YOU NOTES

Most career experts recommend sending thank-you notes. According to Kate Moody, vice president of Human Resources at Oxygen Media, LLC, "I think thank-you notes are still important. It definitely makes an impression when a candidate takes the time to follow up." Only a small percentage of job seekers do—so if you send one, you'll likely stand out.

If you send a note, be prompt and professional. Handwritten is better, but e-mail notes are becoming more acceptable. Either way, a poorly constructed and error-ridden thank-you note will hurt—not help—your chances.

To make your note memorable, mention something specific about the interview—bring up an interesting fact or follow up on a trend you discussed. If she suggested that you do more research on a topic, do it and then mention that in your note. For example:

Dear Ms. Jackson,

Thank you for taking the time to interview me today. I truly feel that my experience as State University student government treasurer has given me the skills critical to success as the executive assistant in the Office of the President.

I was very interested in our discussion of the need to improve the efficiency of your department's project management team. I did some preliminary calculations, and by implementing Computer Conglomerate's "Project Manager 3.2," it appears your employees might save **six hours per week per person**—nearly an entire working day! I would like to be the one to help you achieve this.

I enjoyed meeting you and look forward to hearing from you soon.

Sincerely,

Steve Mitchell

SECOND AND THIRD INTERVIEWS

Sometimes you'll be called back for a second or even a third interview. How will these be different from the first? This time around, expect to spend more time at the company, talk to more people individually and collectively, and have your skills and personality scrutinized more closely.

Be aware that many employers bring in several candidates on the same day to streamline the second interview process. Your challenge is to distinguish yourself from the other candidates.

On your first interview, you probably met with one or two people. This time, be prepared to meet several more over the course of the day, including potential managers, coworkers, and other staff members.

You may meet individually with several people, who will most likely ask you similar questions. Keep your answers consistent but vary your delivery so that your answers don't sound stale or staged. If possible, before the interview get a list of the people you'll be meeting with and do a little research on each one. Then ask questions that show your knowledge of each person.

EXCUSE ME? YOU WANT TO HIRE ME—*NOW?*

It's rare to receive an offer on the spot, but it does happen occasionally. If the feedback is consistently positive over the course of the day, you may get a job offer at the end of the interview. If that happens, don't make a hasty decision. Ask for time to think about it.

Some companies make hiring decisions in a matter of days, but many can take weeks to make their final choice. Be patient, flexible, and ready for an offer or an invitation for yet another interview.

Congratulations—you're now prepared to clear the biggest hurdle in job seeking. No one likes interviews—and that includes the interviewer! Even longtime job seekers struggle with them. So know that you're not alone, and that you now have the tools to make this and every other interview in your future a success!

Recommended Books

Your Job Interview (Barnes & Noble Basics Series) by Cynthia Ingols (Silver Lining Books, ISBN 0760738556, $9.95).

Knock 'em Dead 2005: The Ultimate Job Seeker's Guide (Knock 'em Dead Series) by Martin Yate (Adams Media Corporation, ISBN 1593371063, $14.95).

101 Great Answers to the Toughest Interview Questions by Ron Fry (Delmar Learning, ISBN 156414464X, $11.99).

Sweaty Palms: The Neglected Art of Being Interviewed by Anthony Medley (Ten Speed Press, ISBN 0898154030, $13.95).

Emily Post's Etiquette by Peggy Post (HarperCollins Publishers, ISBN 0066209579, $39.95).

What Not to Wear: For Every Occasion by Trinny Woodall & Susannah Constantine (Riverhead Trade, ISBN 1594480508, $16.00).

Recommended Web Sites

Yahoo! HotJobs Interview Tips:
http://hotjobs.yahoo.com/interview

Equal Employment Opportunity Commission:
www.eeoc.gov

George Mason University Interviewing Strategies for Success:
http://careers.gmu.edu/students/jobhunt/interviewing.html

How To Interview:
www.howtointerview.com

The Professional Image—Article & Interview Archive:
www.theprofessionalimage.net/press.html

Salary.com Mock Job Interviews:
www.job-interview.net/sample/Demosamp.htm

University of San Francisco's Sample Interview Questions:
www.usfca.edu/usf/career/interview_questions.html

CHAPTER 10

Healthy, Wealthy, and Wise: Understanding Salary and Benefits

"Before I forget, Detrick, here's the dental plan."

L et's admit it, you've reached your favorite part of the job-hunting discussion. It's time to talk money. You know, moolah, ducets, benjamins, dinero, cold hard cash. Forget "skills" and "advancement."

Unfortunately, salary for an entry-level employee likely won't let you run out and buy a zippy new sports car or pay off your school loans in one lump sum.

But the good news is that your compensation package is more than your salary–it's your salary *and* your *benefits*—health care, retirement savings, vaca- tion time—even parking spots can be benefits.

So, what type of compensation package can you expect? And when the recruiter hands you a portfolio describing the company's benefits, will you be able to distinguish an attractive offer from a mediocre one?

In this chapter, we'll examine salary and benefits, what's good and what's bad, and how they can work together to provide you security from your new job. You'll need to know all this before you begin to weigh job offers. (In the next chapter, we'll discuss how to negotiate to get more money or better benefits once an offer is on the table.)

hot facts ●●

Money Matters?

In a survey in Yahoo! HotJobs' College Community, a whopping 84 percent of job seekers said that they would take a low-paying job if it meant their student loans would be forgiven.

WHAT ARE YOU WORTH?

To understand what makes a good compensation package for you, you must first determine what *salary* you are worth. Once you know the salary you can command, you can decide which jobs fall into your desired range and could be right for you.

If you already have a specific job you're gunning for, your salary research can come in handy during the interview process, should the subject of salary come up. And it will definitely be helpful if you get a job offer and want to negotiate salary (see chapter 11).

Your salary expectations should be realistic—research the range for your position before you start your job search. Why a range? Because salaries will be fluid according to industry and region. Researching ranges gives you a more

realistic picture of what a position pays. Also, having a range will help you negotiate. You're much more likely to successfully negotiate a salary if you begin with
a range than if you are rigid about a particular number.

There are several tools that can help you understand how salary varies
across job titles and regions:

☼ Salary Wizard lets you research salary by industry and location. You
can find the average U.S. salary for a position or get more detailed
information that takes your experience and employer into account:
http://hotjobs.salary.com.

☼ The Yahoo! HotJobs Salary News tool also offers background on salaries
for various industries as well as a "negotiation clinic": http://swz-hotjobs
.salary.com/salarynews/layoutscripts/salnewsl_display.asp.

☼ The U.S. Department of Labor's *Occupational Outlook Handbook* is also
a very thorough resource for salary information. It is revised every two
years and includes salary data (and much more) on hundreds of jobs:
www.bls.gov/oco/home.htm. The OOH is also available in book form.

Visit the Web sites and directories of professional associations. Often they'll
provide not only salaries for positions in a particular industry, but also ranges
based on geographic location and experience level. Business- and industry-
specific trade magazines and Web sites can offer insights too.

Also, use your network to talk to people who work in the industry you're
targeting. It's not always appropriate to discuss salary—especially with people
you don't know well—so choose your contacts carefully. This is also a great
question to ask in informational interviews—you don't have to ask anyone what
they make specifically, but you can ask about trends and generalities.

UNDERSTANDING YOUR BENEFITS

A standard job offer should include benefits worth about 25 percent or so of
your base salary.

There are many different kinds of benefits; understanding them can help
you make a more informed decision about whether or not a job offer is right for
you. Sometimes a lower salary and better benefits are the way to go. In addition,
companies can usually be more flexible about benefits than salary.

For the remainder of this chapter, we'll examine some of the most common
benefits you will encounter.

Health Care: The Most Important Benefit You Might Never Need

Unfortunately, health care coverage is more expensive now than ever—yet no matter how healthy you are, having health coverage is highly advisable. It only takes one car accident or a slip on an icy sidewalk to make for some very expensive and unavoidable hospital bills. Worse, long-term health costs can reach catastrophic levels overnight in the event of an accident or debilitating disease.

Having a job that offers health care as part of its full-time benefits is the best way to circumvent this issue. Although rising premiums are being passed on to employees, even in large companies, finding a job that offers a company policy or choice of policies is still a great value. Better to have to pay 20 percent of your health coverage than 100 percent.

 **Outside the Box**

Don't Wait Until You're Employed

What can you do for insurance while you conduct your job search? You can find a choice of affordable, individual health care plans at www.ehealthinsurance.com. Or, if you're a recent grad, consider asking your parents to extend your coverage until you find a job, and paying that difference directly to them. If you're living with a significant other, see if his or her company has domestic partnership coverage.

Most important—if you don't have health insurance—remember before you take that skydiving dare from your best buddy or you go flying at 90 mph down that rain-soaked highway that the consequences could not only be painful to your body, but also to your wallet.

Health Care Options

Depending on the size of the company, you'll be given a choice between several different health care plans including versions of the "health maintenance organization" (HMO) and "preferred provider organization" (PPO).

HMOs are health care organizations that are "one-stop shops." If you use an HMO, you will pay less, but you are limited to the HMO's approved doctors and specialists—often located in the same facility. HMOs are often maligned for their rigidity, but they can be a good, inexpensive option for a young, healthy individual.

take a memo

Creating a Budget

Regardless of your salary or age, a household budget is critical to maintaining your economic health. Creating a budget doesn't have to be difficult, as long as you follow some well-established guidelines.

Take into account all of your spending, not just the big-ticket items. It's tempting to streamline the process and only include substantial expenses such as car insurance, electric bills, grocery bills, and your mortgage or your rent. But you spend hundreds of dollars more each month on smaller items that quickly add up: cable TV, Internet access, gas, eating out, magazines, and so forth.

Make a list of expenses and don't generalize—go into detail. Instead of one entry called "Entertainment," itemize it: dining out, sporting events, movie rentals, weekend travel, and such. Track your expenses for at least a month. Use receipts for everything. After the month is over, go over all of your receipts, canceled checks, credit card bills, and the like and discover where your money went.

Then **decide which items you can trim**, and trim them! Why are you paying for a gym membership if you only go three or four times a month? Do you really need to eat out three times a week? At $20 an outing, that's approaching $300 a month. Calculate your spending on your take-home pay, not your gross pay (and never anticipate bonuses—you never know). It sounds pretty cool to say you make $30,000 a year, but after taxes and other deductions, you're really making a little more than $20,000. Spread that out over twelve months, and your wallet's already looking painfully thin.

Vow to save something. If 10 percent isn't possible right now, make it your goal. But save something. If your take-home pay is $20,000 and you vow to save just 5 percent—that's $1,000 after one year. Can you only afford to save 3 percent right now? Fine. Do it. You're setting aside only $23 a paycheck, and your savings will grow to the size of an entire paycheck in just over a year.

Finally, **use the tools available**. There are many books to help you with budgeting, and the Web is a fantastic place to help create your budget. You can find dozens of automated budget programs and software applications by searching on phrases such as "sample budget" and "calculating household expenses." Look at several of them and determine which is the best for you. The results can be sobering—and that's exactly what you need in order to remain realistic.

PPOs allow you to choose from a number of doctors and specialists. They are slightly more expensive, but have more options for your treatment—especially if you need emergency care or care from someone "out of network."

You'll have to do a line-by-line comparison of each plan to see which is best for your circumstance. While you're at it, check the dental and vision benefits as well. For example, some vision plans will cover glasses *and* contacts; others will cover one or the other; and some just cover the exam. Also consider that many plans today include reduced fees for "alternative care" options such as acupuncture and chiropractic care.

Finally, no matter what your health care options, the most critical question for each component is this: *When do they take effect?* In some companies, you're covered the day you walk in the door. At others, there's a ninety-day waiting period. If you're considering multiple employment offers, this could be a deciding factor in choosing one job over another.

Flexible Spending Accounts (FSAs)

These convenient plans allow you to put money aside tax free for medical expenses not covered by your health care plan. These costs include co-pays— the payments you make, usually $15–$25, when you visit a doctor—prescription costs, or the cost of eyeglass frames if your employer does not offer a vision plan. At the end of the year, that money is not counted toward your "net income." In other words, the less you "earn" in the IRS's eyes, the less you are taxed for. Flexible spending accounts can pay off, especially during years in which you anticipate a lot of medical, dental, or vision expenses that will not be covered by insurance. Make sure you understand what the FSA will cover and the conditions for reimbursement. Most FSAs require a receipt and require you to file your expenses by a given deadline—and usually you cannot carry over the balance into the next year.

YOUR FUTURE: RETIREMENT PLANS

It's never too early to begin thinking about retirement. Even though you probably won't be with your first company for the next thirty or more years, you already will need to begin storing away money for your retirement. "Deferred compensation" plans (payment later for work you are doing now) such as defined contribution plans (401[k], profit-sharing, and others) and defined benefit pension plans (traditional pensions) can go a long way toward helping you do that.

Defined Contribution Pension Plans

Defined contribution pension plans give employees a long-term, individual account for retirement benefits derived from their own contributions, tax free, from each paycheck. Defined contribution plans are not guaranteed as many factors can affect their performance—your investment experience, the amount you contribute, stock market fluctuations, and penalties incurred for early withdrawal. These plans include the 401(k), profit-sharing plans, stock bonus plans, and others.

Your company may offer you one or more of these accounts; however, the one you are most likely to encounter at a public or private company is the **401(k) plan**.

A 401(k) plan allows you to contribute a defined percentage of each paycheck, pre-tax, to invest in a variety of mutual funds set up by your company. (It draws its name from Section 401 of the Internal Revenue Code.)

Many companies also match employee 401(k) contributions up to a certain limit. For example, the company might add 50 cents to the account for every dollar you contribute. It may not sound like much now, but this can go incredibly far in helping you save for retirement.

For example, if you earn $30,000 a year, but put $5,000 into a 401(k), your taxable income for the year would be only $25,000. If your company matches 2 percent of your $5,000 in contributions, you're getting an extra $100 free every year to invest in your retirement.

Be aware that your 401(k) earnings are not taxed now, but they will be when you begin making withdrawals, usually after you reach age 59 1/2. If you withdraw earlier, you'll have to pay taxes on the money and, if you are under 55, a 10 percent early withdrawal fee. Still, for the next several decades you will be working, it is widely agreed that the 401(k) is still the best way to save for the future.

Better yet, when you change jobs, you can "roll over" your 401(k) earnings into your next company's 401(k), or your own Individual Retirement Account (IRA), for free.

Defined Benefit Pension Plans (Traditional "Pensions")

Pension plans are funded by your employer and are *guaranteed* to provide a specific amount of money to you monthly after you retire. Even if a company goes bankrupt or otherwise folds, the government, through the Pension Benefit Guarantee Corporation, has ensured that all or most of your pension is guaranteed. Your pension is available to you no matter your age when you begin a job.

What you get when you retire will be based on your salary and the number of years you worked for the company. Generally you become eligible for a pension after one year of service with a company, and you have to be "vested" for a minimum of three to five years before you qualify to receive your pension. Once you retire, you will get your pension whether you have worked at the company five years or thirty-five years. If you leave a job or retire early, you may have a variety of options, depending on the type of plan you have.

STOCK OPTIONS, PROFIT-SHARING, AND YEARLY BONUSES

Perks like these can prove very helpful—or not, since they are tied to a company's overall performance.

Stock options allow you, in lieu of cash, to buy shares of a company below market price. Stock options were especially popular during the Internet boom of the '90s. A handful of companies made even the most entry-level employees rich through stock options, but many people who chose them never saw a dime. Stock options, while risky, can mean a significant boost to your income at a successful company. But be very thorough in your research if stock options are a potential part of your compensation package, and don't count on them as part of your future income.

Profit-sharing (one of the aforementioned "defined contribution" plans) allows employees to earn a portion of a company's pre-tax profits, which the company contributes to a pool to be distributed at the end of the year, according to an employee's base salary.

Yearly bonuses are not accounts, but rather cold, hard cash (sort of). Employees receive a percentage of the company's annual profit—if the company achieves certain goals. It's great to get a big bonus check, but unfortunately, this money is usually taxed heavily.

Individual bonuses, on the other hand, are monies you receive based on your *personal* performance. These are common in careers such as sales. For example, a salesperson might receive a guaranteed 30 percent annual bonus for meeting goals—and this would be part of his compensation package. Again, these can be heavily taxed.

OTHER BENEFITS

Here are the other basic, standard benefits most companies will offer you:

Life Insurance, Short-Term Disability (STD), Long-Term Disability (LTD), Worker's Compensation

Most companies offer forms of these plans. Life insurance is generally a year of your salary payable, along with your accumulated 401(k), pension, and the like, to a beneficiary you designate.

Short-term disability and long-term disability give you percentages of your salary should you be injured, on the job or not, and unable to work for a short or extended period of time.

Worker's compensation is payment for injuries sustained while working or at a work-related event such as a trade show.

Time Off

This includes vacation days, personal days, sick days, and holidays. Standard offerings for entry-level workers are two weeks' paid vacation, a few "personal days"—holidays you take yourself for whatever reason (illness, vacation, just relaxing at home)—and all or most major holidays.

However, don't just look at the number of days allotted per year. Consider when you can start taking advantage of them. How many years of employment until your vacation time (or sick leave) increases? Is it possible to "roll over" any unused days into the next year? Are there "floating holidays" in situations in which you will be called upon to work on national or religious holidays?

You don't need to ask these questions until you have an offer in writing, but it's good to start thinking about them now.

Also, be sure to read carefully all the information the company provides before asking. It likely will answer most of your questions.

Continuing Education

This can be an *extremely* attractive benefit if you're coming into an entry-level position. It's not your goal to stay on the bottom rung, but at bottom-rung pay, it can be difficult to obtain the education necessary to climb that corporate ladder. Tuition reimbursement plans can take the financial sting out of furthering your education.

Companies like to think that sponsoring their employees' education helps them by enhancing the abilities of their employees, and they're half right; in reality, however, you may be getting the better deal because your company is paying to make you more marketable to its competition.

Mind, Body, Soul

Aside from your health care options, does the offer include some extra niceties? Many firms offer free Employee Assistance Programs (EAPs) with, for example, psychological counseling or assistance with caring for an ill family member. Also common are gym memberships, corporate-sponsored getaways, parking and transit discounts, and other perks designed to motivate and invigorate their employees. These benefits can be extremely negotiable.

OTHER CONSIDERATIONS

Before your prospective future employers decided to gamble on you, they did their research—they reviewed your resume, interviewed you (sometimes several times), and compared you to other available candidates. Your scrutiny of them should be no less thorough.

Do some research into the firm, if possible. If you're considering two offers in two different cities, use sites such as Salary.com to compare the cost-of-living in each, especially the housing costs. Check lists such as *Working Mother* magazine's 100 Best Companies for Working Mothers (www.workingmother.com). Even if you're not a mom, these companies are considered by many to offer the country's best all-around benefits. You can compare and contrast what you'll be getting from your new company to these trailblazers.

TAKE HEART—AND *SOME* OF YOUR MONEY

When you get your first check you may be surprised at how little is actually left over for you—your net will probably be somewhere in the area of 60–70 percent of your gross income. But you'll likely recoup some at the end of the year when

Secret Compensation

You might think that "pre-tax" this or "tuition assistance" that doesn't amount to anything, but these are the underappreciated benefits that can stretch your dollar that much further every year. Here's a rough estimate: If you take one class (let's say $500 in tuition), and use flexible spending ($300 for contact lenses and co-pays for physical therapy) and transportation benefits ($200 for commuting) in one year, that's $1,000 you've either saved or do not have to pay taxes on—that's a great bargain!

Employee Assistance Programs: An Employee Assistance Program (EAP) is a counseling and referral program. Employers pay for the programs. So what could be costly professional care is provided free to their workers. Employee Assistance Programs can help you with a wide array of personal, financial, and health care concerns:

- ☼ Child and elder care
- ☼ Credit, financial, and tax issues
- ☼ Legal issues
- ☼ Mental health counseling
- ☼ Parenting skills
- ☼ Substance abuse

Most programs offer a toll-free hotline for assistance. If you prefer a face-to-face meeting, many will also provide referrals to professionals in your area. Many programs also provide confidential emergency counseling around the clock.

Transportation Programs: Companies use transportation programs to help employees reduce their commuting costs. The currency for many of these programs is the transit (or commuter) check, redeemable for public transportation, including buses, subways, and trains. Some companies also cover parking fees.

These programs save employees money by buying transit checks with pre-tax money. Specifically, the company deducts the amount of the transit check from an employee's paycheck before taxes are deducted.

Educational Reimbursements: Companies want the smartest, most skilled workers they can get. That's why some reimburse employees for money they've spent on education.

Most plans require that the education be relevant to a worker's current or future job. For example, many accounting firms will help pay for CPA courses, but not piano lessons. Remember that only courses at an accredited educational institution usually qualify. And some companies require you to be enrolled in a degree program. You may need to earn a minimum grade (say, a "B") for your employer to reimburse you.

take a memo

Meet Mr. FICA

When Jennifer Aniston's character Rachel Green got her first job as a waitress at *Friends* hangout Central Perk, her response to her first paycheck was less than excitement: "Who's FICA? And why does he get all my money?"

You may feel the same way. Consider these "contributions" before you tally your earnings for the next year:

FICA: Under the Federal Insurance Contributions Act, you and your employer share the burden of paying just over 15 percent of your income to Social Security and Medicare—you each pay half (7.65 percent apiece).

Federal/State/City Income Tax: This money is levied by government agencies in order to support the day-by-day workings of your state and local governments.

you do your taxes. (Remember our lesson on pre-tax accounts and how they save you money?) And the more you put into retirement accounts now, the less you'll have to worry in the future!

Recommended Books

401(k)s for Dummies by Ted Benna & Brenda Watson-Newmann (John Wiley & Sons, Inc., ISBN 0764554689, $16.99).

Retire on Less Than You Think: The New York Times Guide to Planning Your Financial Future by Fred Brock (Henry Holt & Company, Inc., ISBN 0805073744, $15.00).

The Wall Street Journal *Guide to Understanding Personal Finance* by Kenneth M. Morris & Virginia B. Morris (Simon & Schuster, ISBN 0743266323, $15.95).

The Complete Idiot's Guide to Personal Finance in Your 20s and 30s by Sarah Young Fisher (Alpha, ISBN 0641589387, $18.95).

Recommended Web Sites

Yahoo! HotJobs Salary & Benefits:
http://hotjobs.yahoo.com/salary

Yahoo! HotJobs Salary Wizard:
http://hotjobs.salary.com

Yahoo! Health—Health Insurance Guide:
http://health.yahoo.com/health/centers/insurance

Assurant Health:
www.assurantdirect.com

About.com's Job Searching Compensation Center:
http://jobsearch.about.com/library/blsalary.htm

Salary.com:
www.salary.com

U.S. Department of Labor's Statistics on Wages, Earnings, and Benefits:
www.bls.gov/bls/wages.htm

U.S. Department of Labor's Health Plans & Benefits:
www.dol.gov/dol/topic/health-plans

***Working Mother* Magazine:**
www.workingmother.com

CHAPTER 11

Is That Your Final Offer?: Negotiating and Deciding on an Offer

"We can't offer you a forty thousand dollar a year job, but perhaps you should consider two twenty thousand dollar a year jobs."

The call you've been eagerly anticipating has arrived. You've been offered your first ever *real job!*

Now you can invite all your friends over to celebrate! Finally, you can call your folks and tell them you won't need help with the rent any longer! Best of all—that third grade teacher who swore you'd never amount to anything? You can track him down at last and tell him he was wrong!

But first you need to sit down and do a bit of careful planning about just what your next move will be. You've been offered a job, and how you proceed from here may determine how well this first job goes!

You may have the offer, but now you'll have to undergo the final details of accepting a new job—whether to say yes or no, negotiation, relocation considerations, paperwork, and timing. Your "work" for this job starts well before your actual "first day."

In this chapter, we'll discuss "sealing the deal" on your new job—or not, if you so choose. Regardless of your decision, handling yourself politely and professionally and educating yourself about compensation (see chapter 10) and negotiation will help you secure a job to celebrate.

MIND YOUR MANNERS

You've been on your best behavior throughout the job searching process—just because you've gotten the offer doesn't mean it's OK to suddenly be carefree. You need to maintain proper etiquette now as you finalize details of your new job. You don't want the employer to question his or her decision to extend you an offer!

You're Not an Employee Yet

Remain professional as you work with the employer on the details of your offer. Yes, they want you, but now is not the time to start acting overconfident or making unreasonable demands. Even at this point, they can change their minds and rescind the offer. Meanwhile, companies grow, change, and are acquired or flat-out fail every day, halting the careers of their current—and future—employees. So don't start doing your happy dance until all the "I"s are dotted and "T"s are crossed. (And even after you are "official," don't let a smug attitude give them a reason to regret their decision.)

Keep It to Yourself

While you are relieved that you have a job offer, don't let that wonderful rush make you reveal something foolish, like, "Wow, I can't believe you guys are gonna pay me that much!" or "You know, I never really did have an offer from that other company." These are your future employers, not your friends (not yet, anyway). Keep your relief confidential and don't let them know you were just eating your last packet of ramen noodles.

Don't Play the Waiting Game

As you ponder whether to accept the job, don't keep employers waiting too long. A few days is acceptable while you consider your decision (even if you already know in your head that all systems are go), so give them an exact date that you'll get back to them with a decision, and do it. One job seeker we spoke to had a summer internship rescinded because she waited too long to accept the offer, and had to go groveling to the employer to get it back. It took weeks of acting like a humble, model employee to get her supervisor to warm up to her after that.

However, it is acceptable to ask for a little time. Most employers will be reasonable, and not expect you to get back to them the next day.

NEGOTIATING

In the previous chapter we outlined the basis of a good compensation package. We also warned you that, given your "newbie" status, you may not be able to negotiate much more than what you've been offered. But you still should consider negotiating (carefully), especially in the area of benefits.

Negotiation may make you think of slick car salesmen in bad suits. But rather than a confrontation, a good negotiation actually is a back-and-forth that eventually achieves common ground with which both parties are happy.

Negotiating makes most people uncomfortable—people don't like to talk about money, much less come right out and ask for it. Being prepared will help make the process a little less painful.

So what can you expect from a negotiation? How do you negotiate? How much do you ask for?

How to Negotiate

You've done your homework regarding realistic salary ranges by visiting salary Web sites and asking folks in the industry, so you should have a range in mind with which you'll be content, keeping in mind the value of the accompanying benefits package.

Memorize this question: *Is there any flexibility here?* Asking about "flexibility" is a tactful way of seeing if you can get more. More money, perhaps, more vacation, more anything.

So when you listen politely to what is being offered, ask just as politely whether or not there is any flexibility. You won't seem pushy, you won't seem greedy. You will seem calm and professional and prepared—exactly the sort of person they want to have working at their company.

Here are some sample situations in which inquiring about flexibility gives the job seeker an advantage:

HR Rep: *Hello Mr. Gonzales. This is Renée with Acme, Inc. I'm calling to let you know that we are extending you an offer to be an event planning assistant in the Marketing Director's Office.*

You: *Thank you. I'm very excited to receive the offer.*

HR Rep: *We're prepared to offer you a starting salary of $27,000 with full benefits.*

You: *Thank you. Considering my four summers' experience in a similar position with Widgets, Inc., and my familiarity with event planning, I was hoping for a salary in the $30,000–32,000 range. Is the salary negotiable?*

HR Rep: *Unfortunately, due to budget restrictions, the salary is non-negotiable.*

You: *I see. Do we have some flexibility in the area of benefits?*

HR Rep: *I think that given your level of qualifications we can offer you a third week of vacation time annually.*

You: *I appreciate your flexibility. I'd like to take the next few days to consider the offer. Can I follow up with you on Wednesday afternoon?*

HR Rep: *Certainly.*

You: *Thank you. I'll call you on Wednesday by 4:00 p.m. with my decision.*

Another possibility:

> **HR Rep:** *Hello Ms. Fisher. This is John with Acme, Inc. I'm calling to invite you aboard as a Web developer.*
>
> **You:** *Wonderful! I'm very happy to hear that.*
>
> **HR Rep:** *We're prepared to offer you a starting salary of $32,000 plus benefits.*
>
> **You:** *Thank you for the offer. Considering my experience coding several award-winning Web sites, I was hoping for a starting salary in the $36,000–38,000 range. Is that possible?*
>
> **HR Rep:** *We like to try and leave some room in starting salaries for growth. However, considering that you do have a level of experience that compares with some of our longer-term developers, we can adjust the salary to $35,000.*
>
> **You:** *Would you be open to $35,000 with a review after six months with the possibility of an increase then?*
>
> **HR Rep:** *I don't see a problem with that.*
>
> **You:** *Thank you. I'm very excited, but I'd like to sleep on it. Can I call you tomorrow?*
>
> **HR Rep:** *That's fine. I look forward to hearing your decision tomorrow.*

These examples were abbreviated, of course, and in real life might take place over several days with some involvement of the hiring manager. In both of these situations, the parties were upfront and polite with their needs. And in both, the job seekers looked for additional ways to increase their compensation package, and asked for time to think about the offer.

You might just get your dream offer the first time around, and if you do, by all means go ahead and take it. Otherwise, you should always be looking for ways to improve the offer—showing the company that you're the smart, confident employee they want on their team.

Bottom line: Think of the negotiation as a discussion, not a debate. Have in mind ahead of time the salary and benefits you need (see chapter 10) and inch your way toward getting them. If you're unsure of anything, simply ask for time to think about it.

Once you feel right about the offer, accept it. If you're still lacking your basic requirements, walk away. You want to work for a company that values its employees and encourages your growth. They'll reflect this even before you work there

THINK Outside the Box

Six Extra Benefits

In lieu of a higher salary, consider asking for:

1. More vacation time. This gives you more paid free time, but is inexpensive to your employer.

2. A title change. Changing a title from "administrative assistant" to "executive assistant" costs your employer nothing, but can be a boost for your resume.

3. Tuition assistance. If your company doesn't offer it, ask if they might explore that for you. If they do offer it, see if you can squeeze an extra class or two out of them.

4. Telecommuting. This perk is becoming much more common and accepted in today's global economy. Ask if it's possible for you—thereby saving you commuting costs.

5. Midyear salary review. You might get your employer to agree to a salary review, and raise should you be exceeding your goals, after six months (be certain to get this perk in writing, so neither of you forget).

6. Relocation expenses. If you're moving across the country or even just across town, ask if the company will pay for all or part of your moving expenses.

in their offer and how they negotiate with you. You, in turn, should also be flexible and open to discussion.

How Far Do You Push?

As we've said, there is value in negotiating, but as a new job seeker you likely don't have much leeway simply because you don't have experience to leverage. In other words, don't push your luck. If you keep pushing back for more and more, you might lose your chance at a job and, at best, you'll annoy your new employer and start your new relationship off on the wrong foot. Only push hard for the things you truly want and need. These are the things that, should you not get them, will allow you to freely walk away from the offer and feel good about doing so.

Decide ahead of time what you absolutely need in your job, salary- and benefit-wise. Also consider the less tangible opportunities and perks—training

take a memo

Negotiating Dos and Don'ts

- ☼ Don't say yes right off the bat—at least take a day or two to think about the offer.
- ☼ Do use research in considering your offer, but...
- ☼ Don't hand out the printouts of salary comparisons to your potential employer.
- ☼ Don't negotiate just for the sake of negotiating—once you reach a deal you're happy with, accept it.
- ☼ Do be confident in your demands, but...
- ☼ Don't be greedy.
- ☼ Do be flexible.
- ☼ Do consider asking for flexibility in benefits—more vacation time, telecommuting, or tuition assistance.

classes, leadership opportunities, commute, casual dress—those things that will make your life easier or help you build your resume for your next job. A job that pays $2,000 less than another, but is thirty minutes closer to your home and offers free training classes sounds like a job well worth taking.

JUGGLING OFFERS

Wouldn't it be amazing if, after all those interviews you sweated through, all those buffed and polished resumes you spread around, suddenly the phone rang not once, but twice with job offers? Seems incredible, but it does happen. If it happens to you, what is the best way to respond?

With more than one job offer in hand you will have to weigh the pros and cons of each:

- ☼ Look closely at what is being offered. Compare the salary and benefits.
- ☼ Think about the long-term career potential. Does one allow opportunity for more—or faster—advancement? Is one a better match for where you want to go in life?

☼ Don't ignore the company reputation. Is one company filled with industry superstars that you can't wait to learn from, while the other one seems to be fading in the business world?

☼ Sit down and imagine accepting one job and think through where your life might be a few years down the road. Do you like the image? Try out the other job in your imagination. How will your life be then?

Don't try to drag companies into a bidding war. You can reveal to each company that you have received another offer as you're negotiating, but be careful not to sound like you're making a threat or issuing an ultimatum. Laura, a job seeker in Washington, DC, was working at a job she had outgrown, and received an offer from an up-and-coming dotcom. Her employer found out about the new job and offered Laura a raise to keep her on. Her confidence boosted, she attempted to get the new company to improve their offer by a few thousand dollars, and aggressively used her current employer's raise as a bargaining chip. Eventually, she pushed too far, and she lost the new opportunity entirely. While she had gained a higher salary with her original employer, after six months Laura ended up quitting because she was so dissatisfied with her working conditions, and she had to take a lower-paying job. Ultimately, Laura discovered that a few thousand dollars was not worth sacrificing a great opportunity.

You may get lucky and one or both companies might indeed raise their offer for you. Just remember that it's a risky venture, and don't keep going back and back again to the companies. Make up your mind in a reasonable amount of

take a memo

When Everybody Wants You

Having one or more job offers in hand gives you the opportunity to call back a company with which you've interviewed and you'd really prefer. Talk to the HR person there from a position of strength. Say that you've been offered a job, but prefer the idea of working for her company, and would like to find out if you are still under consideration. It might well be the extra push required to move you up on her list and result in a job offer. Or perhaps, a few months or years from now when another position comes up, you will be on her hot list to call.

time. And don't bluff and say you have another offer when you don't—you'll risk losing the real offer, and then you'd feel like a fool. A jobless fool.

CAN I THINK ABOUT THIS FOR A FEW DAYS?

Even if you have just been offered the job of your dreams, this is a good time to pause and consider your next move. No one will be surprised or offended if you ask for a few days to consider the offer. But there are also some things you shouldn't say. For example:

"I'm waiting to hear from another company."

"I need to check with my friends to see what they think."

"I just woke up and I need to think about this when I am a little more alert."

Do say:

"I'd like to sit down and think this through."

"I need some time to think more about the offer."

"This is a big decision and I'd like a few days to consider it."

Remember the etiquette warning: Always be respectful, professional, and polite in how you phrase your questions and conversation. Don't make the mistake of thinking that, once you have an offer, you no longer need to be on your best behavior.

GRACEFUL WAYS TO CLOSE (BUT NOT SHUT) THE DOOR

Saying "no" without burning a bridge is an art form, one that you would do well to master early in your career. This is business, of course, and the company you are turning down will understand that and not take it personally if you handle it in a businesslike manner.

There are any number of reasons why you might turn down an offer, and they are your business alone. Maybe the salary wasn't good enough, maybe the commute was too long, or maybe you've taken another job.

However, you want the hiring manager to respect and remember you in the future—especially if you really liked that particular company. You never know when a new manager might replace the one with whom you didn't hit it off; or when that same company could launch an entire new division next year that handles exactly the work you are looking for. Or, for whatever reason, your new job simply may not turn out to be what you thought.

Meeting the recruiter in person is not necessary; speaking by phone is fine. However, by no means decline an offer by e-mail. This shows that you didn't care enough about his offer to do more than tap out a few sentences.

Call the recruiter—not the hiring manager—with your news, and within the decision time you specified. Say that you've given his "generous" offer "much consideration." While you are "honored" that he would select you, you have decided not to accept at this time.

Depending on your reason for declining, you might even ask that they keep your resume on file—especially in cases where you liked the company, but were lukewarm about the job itself.

What to Say. First, you don't have to give an exact reason, but you do need to say something. For example:

"I don't feel this position is the right fit for me at this time."

"After much thought, I feel my skills would be better utilized in XYZ capacity. Please keep my resume on file if that position becomes available."

"I feel that in order to achieve my goal of obtaining a position in marketing, I should focus my search there."

If you have taken another job, you do not need to offer that information—especially if it's with a competitor. You do *not* want to say something like the following:

"I don't think I'd get along with the hiring manager."

"Your salary can't touch what I'm getting at Company X."

"I don't like the commute."

These reasons might be true, but you don't need to share them. Remember that networking thing? You never know when you and the recruiter or hiring manager might cross paths again someday.

ACCEPTING AN OFFER

Saying "yes" to an offer is simple at first—call the recruiter and verbally accept the offer.

It's the aftermath that can be very frustrating—you're ready to get going on your new job, after all—what's all this "orientation" stuff about? It's all necessary to add you to a company's roster.

Setting a Start Date

Once a company offers you a job, chances are they want to get you in as soon as possible. You, however, may need some time to prepare.

First, you may already be working. Professional etiquette dictates that you should give an employer two weeks' notice when you leave a job. Employers generally understand and accept this courtesy and are wailing to wait. After all, they hope that one day, if you leave, you'll show them the same respect.

Also, you may need some time to relax so you can start your new job fresh. Try to set a start date that allows you time to wrap up your personal affairs—moving, visiting family and friends, setting up bank accounts and utilities, and so forth.

Paperwork

It may be months before you handle in your real job the amount of paperwork you're about to take on to get started with a company. The sooner you get it done, the sooner you can get those little things like your name badge, your desk, your paycheck...

Offer letter. While most job offers will be given verbally, either at the end of a second interview or over the phone, you should always make sure you get the offer in writing, usually in the form of the offer letter.

The offer letter protects you and your prospective employer by stating in writing what you both expect to happen with your hiring, such as:

- ☼ The exact position you are being offered
- ☼ Your start date
- ☼ Your salary
- ☼ Pay periods the company uses (twice a month, every two weeks, every week, and so on)
- ☼ Benefits package
- ☼ Supervisor

You might also ask if there is a written job description that could be attached to the job offer letter, again so that both you and your new employer know what to expect. Be warned, however, that the formal offer will be contingent on you passing whatever other tests might be left (see page 169).

Contract. Similar to the offer letter, an "employment contract" is a more formal (and probably lengthier) legal document that states the rights, obligations, and expectations of the company and the individual. Few first-time jobs will require you to sign a job contract; these usually come into play later in your career. If your job offer includes an employment contract, do take the time to read it carefully and consult an attorney if you have any questions.

Noncompetes. You might be asked to sign a noncompete agreement that prohibits you from working in the same field for a length of time after you leave your job. You will probably need to sign it as a condition of employment, but if you don't feel comfortable about it, ask an attorney's advice. Keep in mind that this could severely limit your employment options for a period of time if things don't work out and you want to seek a similar job with a different employer.

Nondisclosure agreements. A Nondisclosure Agreement (NDA) is a contract between you and the company stating that you will not divulge company information to anyone. NDAs are standard in many industries in which information and business practices are closely guarded. If it is a condition of employment, you will need to sign it, but again, seek out the advice of an attorney if you don't understand the implications or if you feel uncomfortable. NDAs also go by other names such as "confidentiality agreements" and "confidential disclosures."

HR forms. Health care choices, life insurance, payroll, 401(k)—remember all those snazzy benefits you were offered? Now you have to sign up for all of them. Be especially careful to get these forms in on time—you do not want to miss enrolling in a health care plan and have to wait until the following quarter to sign up, or miss out on a month's worth of company 401(k) matching funds because you lost the form.

Some paperwork of your own. You've received a letter formalizing the job offer; now, you might respond with a letter of your own, accepting the offer. It's a nice touch, from a professional standpoint, and gives you the chance to put in writing what you understand the job to be.

What should you say in your acceptance letter? Once again, be as polite and respectful as possible (this is not the place to be flip) and restate what you understand to be the job title and major responsibilities, salary and benefits package, and your starting date.

Are you done yet? As long as you are in the letter-writing mode, why not keep going and send out letters to the folks who've helped you in your job search? This is the perfect time to thank them for their help, inform them of your success, and solidify a good impression. Who knows—you might someday need their help again, and wouldn't it be nice if they remembered you as that polite person who sent a thank-you note? Send a note of thanks that includes the news of your new job to:

- ☼ College career center staff who were helpful in your job search
- ☼ Networking contacts you used among family and friends
- ☼ HR people at the companies you interviewed with
- ☼ Industry folks who helped mentor and advise you

OTHER ODDS AND ENDS (THAT MAY SEEM ODD)

Often today job offers are *contingent* on some important, and perhaps slightly worrisome, "tests." However, drug tests, and credit and background checks, are common and legal.

Drug Tests

Drug tests are not mandatory in all companies or in all industries. If a drug test is required, the recruiter will give you the necessary information. However, setting up the appointment will likely be your responsibility. Test results will be sent directly to the employer. An employer can't force you to take a drug test but if you refuse, you will likely no longer be considered for employment.

Credit Checks

When you first filled out an official application for the job (not your response to the job ad), you may have signed a piece of paper giving the recruiter permission to run a credit check on you. The reason is that companies may have doubts about hiring someone who has made repeated bad financial decisions in her personal life, especially if she will be handling a budget.

Fortunately, at this point in your career you have not yet built much of a credit history. You likely, however, have student loan debt. This will not hurt you in a credit check; however, you should already be taking steps toward paying it off, or it could become a credit burden in the future. For help learning about your credit or getting out of loan debt, consult:

- ☼ The Federal Trade Commission's Credit Scoring:
  www.ftc.gov/bcp/conline/pubs/credit/scoring.htm
- ☼ Sallie Mae: www.salliemae.com

Background Checks

Another form you may have signed when you applied was a permission form to perform a background check on you. These checks are carried out by an outside agency, which looks into such things as your previous addresses, college and work history, and whether you have a criminal record.

WELCOME ABOARD!

Okay, *now* you can relax. You've been offered a job, carefully weighed what it will mean to your future, accepted the offer, and have a start date in hand. So go celebrate, already. Your career is off and running.

Recommended Books:

Getting to Yes: Negotiating Agreement Without Giving In by Roger Fisher & William Ury (Penguin, ISBN 0140157352, $15.00).

The Art of Negotiating by Gerard I. Nierenberg (Barnes & Noble Books, ISBN 156619816X, $5.98).

Get Paid What You're Worth: The Expert Negotiators' Guide to Salary and Compensation by Robin Pinkley & Gregory Northcraft (St. Martin's Press, ISBN 031230269X, $13.95).

The Good Girl's Guide to Negotiating by Leslie Whitaker & Elizabeth Austin, (Little, Brown & Company, ISBN 0316601470, $13.95).

Recommended Web Sites

University of San Francisco's Career Services Center Guide to Negotiating Salary & Benefits:
www.usfca.edu/usf/career/salary.html

Yahoo! HotJobs Top Candidate Background Check:
http://hotjobs.choicetrust.com

Yahoo! HotJobs Relocation:
http://hotjobs.yahoo.com/relocation

The Federal Trade Commission's Credit Scoring:
www.ftc.gov/bcp/conline/pubs/credit/scoring.htm

Florida State University's Etiquette Survival Guide:
www.career.fsu.edu/ccis/guides/etiquette.html

I've Got a Job Offer, What Now?:
www.rose-hulman.edu/careerservices/joboffer.htm

12

Ready, Set, Go!:
Getting Started at Your New Job

Congratulations—you have just accomplished what may well be the biggest achievement of your life thus far—your first real, full-time job!

Just think—thousands, maybe *millions* of people of all ages and levels of experience look for jobs every day, and you found one! This is no small feat.

You probably have hundreds of little details to work out as you get ready to start your job. But now—and always—you need to keep the big picture in mind. Although you haven't even seen your shiny new cubicle yet, you should already be thinking, however distantly, about your *next job*.

Why? Because this job, and every other job that follows (and believe us, there will be more) is a step along your career path. Some steps will be smooth and close together. Others will be jagged and far apart, with the occasional spouse, or relocation, or advanced degree crossing your path.

The steps on your path may be completely unrelated. As long as your path leads you in (mostly) an upward direction of fulfillment throughout your life, that is what matters.

Notice we said "fulfillment" not "salary." Oh, we won't kid you, money is definitely important, and as your career path twists and turns, your salary might likely rise and fall with it.

But "fulfillment"—that feeling that you are using your own unique talents to create your personal niche in the world, is far more valuable than any paycheck. As you proceed through your career you should always be thinking of how you can prepare yourself for your next move. You just took your first step!

Your first job will provide you with tools and opportunities to develop your career—you need to take advantage of them. In this chapter, we'll look at how to make the most of this job and how to build upon it to prepare you for an even better one when you're ready to move up.

STRUT YOUR STUFF

The minute you begin your new job, you have the opportunity to really show why they hired you. Despite paperwork, orientation, human resources manuals, getting your employee badge, and yet more paperwork, you can already begin to make good impressions on everyone from your new coworkers to the security guard.

For example, make an effort to remember people's names. Pay attention during your training and ask thoughtful questions. Begin to identify people who can help you when you have a question. Be friendly and upbeat, even if you're nervous.

Then roll up your sleeves and learn everything you can about your new job—and others' jobs as well. The more you know the easier your job will be, and the more effective an employee you'll be. Show your coworkers and manager that you can succeed despite your newbie status, and show that where you lack skills you'll do what it takes to learn them.

Also, don't be afraid of a challenge. Volunteer to take part in projects that might be "over your head"—not only will you demonstrate a good attitude, but you can also learn something that will help you get promoted or find that you are better suited for a different area of work.

hot facts •

Make the Most of Your First Job

The goal of most job seekers (65 percent) is to gain experience during their first jobs. Satisfaction and money were next in importance (17 and 16 percent, respectively), according to a survey in Yahoo! HotJobs' College Community.

NURTURE YOUR NETWORK

Now that you've gotten a job it may be tempting to let go of the contacts in your network. Don't! You've worked hard to build it—and you'll need it when you look for your next job. The contacts you are making now can be the same ones that lead to opportunities one, two, ten years from now. Stay in touch with them.

Let everyone in your network know that you've found employment—but continue to seek their help and advice. And be a resource for them as well—when you see a job opening at your new company, pass it along. It's the right thing to do, and you might even score a "referral bonus" cash payout from HR as well.

Most important, you'll need your network as you progress through this job and into others.

Look to expand your network at your new job. Mentors, managers, coworkers, friends of managers and coworkers—meet people, get their e-mail addresses, do what you can to add them to your network—and yourself to theirs. It can pay off repeatedly as you follow your career path.

MANUFACTURE A MENTOR

Luke Skywalker, Harry Potter, Buffy the Vampire Slayer—they all had something in common.

No, not magic powers, but a great mentor! Someone who could answer their questions, teach them skills, show them the ropes (or basic spells...).

A mentor is a more seasoned employee, Jedi, wizard, whatever, who can help you navigate workplace situations that you have likely not encountered before.

Many larger companies have formal mentoring programs, but you'll likely have to try and find a mentor on your own. A mentor can be someone within your company—your manager, your manager's manager, or even an employee in a completely different department. In a formal program you might meet with your mentor once or twice a month to go over your questions and concerns. If there is no mentor program, perhaps there is a "buddy" program, in which you are matched with another employee who can answer your questions. If there is no formal program at all, ask at work and among your network for help in finding a mentor.

In addition, a mentor doesn't have to be someone you work with—a former professor or even a favorite relative can be a mentor. However, the best mentors are not simply people you admire, but those who can help you advance in your career as well. Don't be afraid to ask them questions—learn from their mistakes, so you won't make as many of your own.

CONTINUING YOUR EDUCATION

As you begin your new job, be open to every learning opportunity you can get.

Keep an eye out for formal learning opportunities, both at work and at outside institutions. When there are training classes in software related to your job, take them. When there are speakers on a topic related to your field, go sit front and center. When there are conventions and events for your industry, ask if you can go. Even if the answer is "no," a manager won't fault you for wanting to learn everything you can. Your attitude alone will score you points.

Finally, if your company offers tuition assistance, use it. Start work on that master's degree, MBA, associate's degree in accounting. Not only can you use your learning to advance at your current job, but you can use it to get an even better job in the future, too. And with your company paying for all or most of it, you may have a free advanced degree before you pay off the loans for your *undergrad* efforts!

From the Desk of

William D. Novelli
CEO, AARP

Always recognize that your greatest asset is your reputation, regardless of your career path or the jobs you will hold. I learned early on that integrity, positive business goals and business practices, and a strong sense of ethics and values are the best protection for your reputation. These intangibles guide the way we do business, as well as the way we live our lives. They represent our character.

I also believe in the value of social marketing—a concept that has continued to develop for me over time. Basically, it's applying market strategies to bring visibility and awareness to social issues. It keeps us focused on achieving the greater good for all of society, as well as committed to social responsibility.

We all possess the power to make it better, as individuals; collectively, we have that power by joining together to reach common goals and by improving the quality of life for all people.

Early in my career, I marketed laundry detergent, fabric softener, children's breakfast cereal, and margarine for Unilever. Later, I worked for the Peace Corps and CARE, cofounded a PR firm, and was president of the Campaign for Tobacco-Free Kids. Today, I'm privileged to lead the nation's largest organization for people fifty and older. Throughout these many opportunities, I've discovered that marketers and advertisers often don't recognize the power of market segments.

Make it your business to know your market, your audience—the people you want to reach. Then serve them, no matter what your job or career path, with character, integrity, and purpose. And remember to take time for yourself and your family. Never live to work. Life is precious and so are the people you love. Work hard, but balance your work and your personal time. You'll have no regrets.

take a memo

Freshmen Again

Well, once again you've gone from top of the ladder to bottom rung. You're a freshman again. As a new employee, you not only have people to meet and skills to learn for your job, but "workplace" skills that just have to come with life experience. Here are a few tips, however, to give you a head start:

Employee Don't Phone Home: Don't make or receive unnecessary personal calls on your office phone, or even your cell phone, at work unless you're on your lunch break. And by all means, don't make unnecessary long distance calls from your office phone. Not only is your company charged, but as a new employee, all eyes are on you—and that means anyone, not just your manager.

Easy on the E-mail: Because e-mail and Internet browsers belong to the company, in most cases, your manager can not only "spy" on what you're writing, but can fire you for it too—legally. Also avoid dubious Web sites, music downloads, and any file that even remotely has the slightest, teeniest, minute *whiff* of a virus.

Breakroom Breakdown: Every office has its gossip and banter when coworkers get together. In its most innocent state, gossip can build camaraderie and maintain morale, but resist the impulse to get embroiled in someone's personal affairs. Also, refrain from cursing and absolutely do not tell off-color jokes, even to the most "laid-back" individual—you never know who might be listening nearby.

Interoffice Dating: The safe answer is just don't do it. But if you start a job and find yourself completely head over heels for the cute assistant down the hall, at least make sure you are both on the same employment level—you do not want to date someone senior or subordinate to you as it creates power struggles and could have a bearing on your career path, unfair as that may be. Consider that, at worst, you could face potential lawsuits, and at best, marry your coworker—and then see him every single day for the rest of your life. Or break up and see him every single day of your life. It's your call.

Bon Voyage!

Finding a job has been the hard part—now the fun begins! You're starting a journey that will last the rest of your life and has so many possible twists and turns. You'll be amazed in ten years or more when you look back at all you've accomplished, and how it all began with this first job. Hopefully, this book has helped make finding it a little easier, and you'll count on Yahoo! HotJobs again when you're ready to take that next big step!

Recommended Books

Don't Sweat the Small Stuff at Work: Simple Ways to Minimize Stress and Conflict While Bringing out the Best in Yourself and Others by Richard Carlson (Hyperion, ISBN 0786883367, $11.95).

The Etiquette Advantage in Business: Personal Skills for Professional Success by Peggy Post & Peter Post (HarperCollins Publishers, ISBN 0062736728, $35.00).

The Pathfinder: How to Choose or Change Your Career for a Lifetime of Satisfaction and Success by Nicholas Lore (Simon & Schuster, ISBN 0684823993, $15.00).

What Color Is Your Parachute? 2005: A Practical Guide for Job-Hunters and Career Changers by Richard Nelson Bolles (Ten Speed Press, ISBN 1580086152, $17.95).

Recommended Web Sites

Yahoo! Health—Work/Life:
http://health.yahoo.com/health/centers/work_life

About.com—Quitting Your Job:
http://careerplanning.about.com/od/quittingyourjob/

Professionals In Transition Support Group:
www.jobsearching.org

U.S. Department of the Interior's Online Career Transition Course:
www.doi.gov/octc/strategy.html

U.S. Department of Labor:
www.dol.gov

INDEX

ARTIST CREDITS
for Chapter Openers

Chapter 1: Barbara Smaller
Chapter 2: Mick Stevens
Chapter 3: Henry Martin
Chapter 4: Mike Twohy
Chapter 5: Peter Mueller
Chapter 6: Robert Mankoff
Chapter 7: Frank Modell
Chapter 8: Peter Steiner
Chapter 9: Michael Maslin
Chapter 10: Leo Cullum
Chapter 11: Frank Cotham
Chapter 12: Tom Cheney